CLASS WARFARE
IN THE
INFORMATION AGE

CLASS WARFARE
IN THE
INFORMATION AGE

Michael Perelman

St. Martin's Press
New York

ISBN 0-312-22477-X

Library of Congress Cataloging-in-Publication Data

Perelman, Michael.
    Class warfare in the information age / Michael Perelman.
        p.   cm.
    Includes bibliographical references and index.
    ISBN 0-312-17758-5 (cloth)   0-312-22477-X (pbk)
    1. Information society. 2. Information technology—Social
aspects. 3. Social classes. 4. Social conflict.   I. Title.
HM221.P44   1998
303.6—dc21   97-53280
                                                            CIP

Book design by Orit Mardkha-Tenzer

First published in hardcover in the United States of America in 1998
First St. Martin's paperback edition: December 1999
10 9 8 7 6 5 4 3 2 1

Contents

Preface to the Paperback Edition

I was probably insufficiently alarmed when I was writing this book. Today, the patent system is running amok. The Patent and Trademark Office is awarding a torrent of far-reaching privileges that threaten to create new imbalances in our society. Firms routinely win patents for "business practices," which are nothing more than mundane ways of doing business, such as the way that offers are to be made on the Internet. The end result of these patents will be a morass of litigation for which the public will ultimately pay. The pace at which firms win patents for life forms is accelerating. The supposedly nearby completion of the Human Genome Project suggests ever more ominous outcomes.

Universities are focusing more and more on winning patents rather than teaching for furthering science. In 1998, the University of California alone won 395 patents. In its zeal to profit from these patents, the university is offering to sell patents to potential licensees over the Internet.

In the educational front, the University of California, Berkeley has virtually merged its Department of Plant and Microbial Biology with Novartis, a huge Swiss transnational corporation specializing in biotechnology and chemicals.

Since this book first appeared, government agencies are expanding their rights to intrude further into our electronic and voice communications. The current administration equates privacy rights, such as the ability to encrypt email, as an open invitation to crime and terrorism. Worrisome information about the government's technical ability to gather information has come to light. The recent revelations about the Echelon system indicate capabilities that would have previously been confined to the realm of science fiction.

The recent elimination of restrictions on financial corporations to link together banking, insurance and other financial services with industry greatly enhances their ability to gather huge databases of private information.

I wish that I could report great advances in the potential of new communication technologies to defend freedom from further corporate intrusions. Perhaps the one positive sign was the use of the Internet to stop, or at least delay, the Multilateral Agreement on Investments, which would have provided corporations the right to override local, state, or even federal laws that inconvenience them in the name of preventing restrictions on trade.

Introduction

The title of this book is intentionally provocative. Mention of class struggle evokes images of a grimy age in which bygone captains of industry callously oppressed armies of overworked and underpaid proletarians. This dark portrait of class conflict stands in sharp contrast with the glorious promise of an information age. Supposedly, with the help of modern computer and telecommunication technologies, we can look forward to life in a well-educated society in which anybody with even a modicum of intelligence and discipline can enjoy a more than comfortable existence.

Unfortunately, the reality of the information age falls considerably short of the futuristic vision of the information age. In fact, the imaginary dystopias of science fiction seem to be closer to the truth than the fantasies of the champions of the coming information age.

Despite our wondrous technological achievements, everybody is grumbling today. The rich complain that they pay too much in taxes and nobody wants to work for them at a reasonable wage. The poor have trouble finding work. When they do, their wages often fail to lift them out of poverty. The middle class rightly fears that their prosperity is precarious, knowing that their numbers are rapidly diminishing.

In this contentious environment, blame is cast about with abandon. Multitudes of groups are singled out for abuse: dark-skinned people, welfare recipients, immigrants, government bureaucrats, homosexuals, atheists, fundamentalists, and vague, but ominous forces that secretly plot against world government. Occasionally, one even finds mention of giant corporations.

This book attempts to make sense of this welter of conflicting claims and accusations in the context of the information revolution. Chapter 1, entitled "A Skeptical Reading of the Information Revolution," attempts to put the information revolution in perspective. This chapter makes the case that the information revolution is overblown. I show that despite the ubiquitous computer, our usual measures of the quantitative growth of the information economy suffer from numerous biases.

The second chapter, "Classes and the Information Revolution," continues with the deflation of the concept of an information revolution. Here we see that, despite the rise in information technologies, we are doing little to lay the educational groundwork for a real information economy. In addition, most new employment falls outside of the information economy in the low wage service sectors. Finally, for the most part, the information technologies are not being applied to improve the quality of life. Instead, they are being used to perfect command and control processes, often at the expense of the well-being of workers.

The third chapter, "Information and the Labor Process," expands on the theme of the use of information technologies for command and control. This chapter shows that if we are to enjoy the full potential of an information economy, we need to use information processes in our workplaces in an entirely new fashion. We must develop and engage the technological potential of all employees rather than use information technologies to strengthen the control of management over labor.

Chapter 4, "The Contradiction of Exploited Informational Labor," describes the brittleness of the new technologies. A single error in a massive computer program can cause a disaster, in many cases even life-threatening consequences. Under such conditions, command and control management is self-defeating. This chapter also discusses how and why economists have been slow to realize how information technologies require a new understanding of the relationship between labor and management.

Chapter 5, "Panopticism," shows why the use of information as a commodity necessitates a more intrusive government to protect intellectual property rights. This chapter also indicates how the new information technologies are also used to exert control of the general population outside of the workplace.

Chapter 6, "Information as a Commodity," analyzes how the growth of intellectual property rights undermines the growth of science and technology, thereby restricting the potential of the information economy.

Chapter 7, "Markets and Informational Efficiency," takes on Hayek's idea that markets are conducive to informational efficiency. Among other things, this chapter uses a brilliant but neglected insight of Hayek's to show how markets are antithetical to efficiency. This chapter also demonstrates why markets are poorly equipped to manage the production and exchange of information.

Chapter 8, "Toward a Real Information Age," attempts to point to ways in which the technologies of the supposed information revolution could be turned to good purpose.

A Preview

Although I am an economist, my professional training did little to prepare me to understand the information age. In fact, like most students of economics, I heard almost nothing of conflict, except for complaints about the galling differences between those who accept the prevailing dogma and the ignorant masses who do not.

This simplistic predisposition to assume that competitive market forces somehow automatically induce social harmony dates back at least as far as Adam Smith's *Wealth of Nations*, published more than two centuries ago. At the time, Smith postulated:

> It is not from the benevolence of the butcher, the brewer, or the baker that we expect our dinner, but from their regard to their own interest. We address ourselves, not to their humanity but to their self-love, and never talk to them of our own necessities but of their advantages. (Smith 1776, I. ii. 2, pp. 26-7)

Unfortunately, not only has economics failed to progress since the far simpler days of Adam Smith; it has actually regressed. On a more subtle level than his oft cited words about butchers and bakers, Smith clearly understood class conflict in a way in which modern economists rarely, if ever, appreciate. After all, Smith himself lived in an age of serious class struggle. Most of his well-to-do contemporaries believed, with good cause, that Britain was on the verge of a civil war (Thompson 1963). Smith himself went to great lengths in delineating the distinctly different interests of landlords, workers, peasants, and merchants.

Despite the tumult of the time, Smith himself was optimistic that the market would eventually defuse the conflict between the contending classes. He prophesied that the market would somehow cut the idle rich down to size, while simultaneously lifting the hard working poor into comfortable middle class affluence and culture. Through this route, class struggle would vanish and society would become harmonious sometime in the future.

Although Smith's views about social harmonies are far more complex than those of the typical economist of today, judging from the contentious world around us, we must recognize that Smith was far off the mark in his predictions about the future demise of class struggle. The market seems to have done little to transcend the conflict between classes. Anger and hatred are more common than ever. True, the generic classes of capitalists and workers seem inappropriate today, but only because these great classes have fragmented into smaller grouplets of angry people.

The flowery rhetoric of the information age rekindles Adam Smith's tattered vision of social harmonies. Popular writers, such as Alvin Toffler and George Gilder, propose that the widespread availability of information at modest prices will topple the old industrial structure, allowing anyone with a modicum of ambition to prosper as an entrepreneur. According to such authorities, we have no cause to grumble. All we need to do is to dismantle the Second Wave institutions of the state and grab hold of the profitable entrepreneurial opportunities that await us (Harvey 1995, p. 9).

I will take issue with the simplistic optimism of the information age as an epoch in which information replaces labor and material goods. I will argue that this conception of the information age is overblown at best. However, to the extent that we are entering an information age—and surely information is becoming increasingly important in our economy— the process will reinforce existing class structures rather than bring us to a classless, harmonious world.

The real information revolution is not that information is suddenly becoming important. Information has always been important. The revolutionary aspect of the information age is the treatment of information as a commodity in ways that would have been unimaginable only a few decades ago.

While the technologies of the information age greatly expand the economic potential of society, the benefits of these technologies are far from equally distributed. In fact, these changes will throw many of the less fortunate into destitution.

The failure of technology to deliver on its promise is not a new phenomenon by any means. For example, well before the information age, as the Industrial Revolution drew to a close, John Stuart Mill despaired of the yawning gap between technology's potential and its effect on the masses of the population. "Hitherto it is questionable if all the mechanical inventions yet made have lightened the toil of any human being" (Mill

1848; 3, p. 756). Mill was hardly a casual observer. On the contrary, he was widely considered to be the foremost economist of his day and his *Principles of Political Economy* was the most influential text for decades.

Let me warn you at this time that my book is neither about classes nor technology as such. It does concern the reciprocal relationship between class structure and technology. I chose to analyze this subject because I am convinced that a proper understanding of classes and technology is crucial for making intelligent choices about the kind of society that we create for ourselves.

In this respect, I show why an information age is inconsistent with a market system. Specifically, I will discuss why the rules of the market impede the production and distribution of knowledge and information. I will also investigate the manner in which markets contaminate both the flow of and the application of information.

1

A Skeptical Reading of the Information Revolution

Misleading Rhetoric of the Information Economy

We are awash in a jumble of contradictory rhetorical images about the nature of this so-called information economy. Much that we read would have us believe that modern capitalist economies are now entering an information age.

Typically, we get the impression of an information age from the ubiquitousness of information technology. Indeed, computers are everywhere. A typical car today has more computer-processing power than the first lunar landing craft had in 1969 (*The Economist* 1996a, p. 4).

Major corporations are quick to redefine themselves within the context of the impending information revolution. More than a decade and a half ago in 1982, the American Express Corporation responded to its inclusion in the Dow Jones Industrial Index with a proclamation of that firm's growing infatuation with the increasing role for information:

> [O]ur product is information. . . . Information that charges airline tickets, hotel rooms, dining out, the newest fashions, and even figures mailing costs for a travel magazine; information that grows money funds, buys and sells equities and manages mergers; information that pays life insurance annuities. (Schiller 1988, p. 27)

Manuel Castells puts an academic gloss on this new vision of the business world. After making the relatively reasonable observation that we are witnessing the transformation of corporations into networks (Castells 1996, p. 165), he becomes almost rhapsodic, proclaiming that "the network enterprise . . . transforms signals into commodities by processing knowledge" (Castells 1996, p. 172).

Castells's idea of a commercial alchemy that "transforms signals into commodities by processing knowledge" is worthy of note because Castells himself is usually careful to warn against the chimera of an information economy. He provides extensive data to demonstrate that a vibrant economy requires that information processing remain linked with traditional economic activities (Castells, pp. 209ff). Yet the very notion of an information economy is so seductive that Castells finds himself swept up with the bizarre rhetoric of the information economy.

Lesser minds are even less able to resist offering up the happy imagery of a utopian information society in which we will all live in comfort and ease. According to this comforting Tofflerian view, except for a possible smattering of individuals who perversely refuse to take advantage of the plethora of educational opportunities, we might imagine that all of us will soon live happily together as a community of symbolic analysts. Lest you think that I am going off the deep end with this characterization of those left behind, let me turn your attention to a *Wall Street Journal* writer of this persuasion:

> One would imagine that the poor would get all the information they want as things stand now and in many cases, even resist the efforts of school, libraries and the information media to make them better informed. Indeed, that resistance often helps to explain why they are poor. (Melloan 1994; emphasis added)

Bill Gates, the head of Microsoft Corporation, adds another dimension to the rhetoric of the information economy. He promises us that the new information age technologies "will carry us into a new world of low-friction, low-overhead capitalism, in which market information will be plentiful and transaction costs low. It will be a shopper's heaven" (Gates 1995, p. 158).

Perhaps nobody goes as far as George Gilder, who begins his book, *Microcosm,* with the extravagant claim:

> The central event of the twentieth century is the overthrow of matter. In technology, economics, and the politics of nations, wealth in the form of physical resources is steadily declining in value and significance. The powers of mind are everywhere ascendant over the brute force of things. (Gilder 1989, p. 18)

Following Gilder's logic, with the elimination of physical barriers to affluence, the abolition of poverty should be an easy matter.

Others turn the productivity of the information age on its head, warning of the ominous implications of an impending end of work, where all too many will be left adrift in a society that no longer needs their labor (Rifkin 1995). While information technologies may eliminate the need for certain types of work, a hasty glance around us suffices to find pressing demands for all sorts of work. Our infrastructure lies in disrepair. Schools and hospitals are decaying. Centuries of environmental neglect call out for massive remediation. Concern about the end of work is premature, to say the least.

Lest we become carried away with the extravagant claims about the revolutionary nature of the coming information age, we should keep in mind that announcements of the impending information age are hardly new. Consider the following futuristic fantasy from Edward Ross's *Social Psychology*, published in 1908:

> Presence is not essential to mass suggestion. Mental touch is no longer bound up with physical proximity. With the telegraph to collect and transmit the expressions and signs of the ruling mood, and the fast mail to hurry to the eager clutch of waiting thousands the still damp sheets of the morning daily, remote people are brought, as it were, into one another's presence. (Ewan 1996, p. 71; citing Ross 1908, p. 63)

Certainly the telegraph and the circulation of daily newspapers had an effect on society, but not nearly as profound as Ross had anticipated.

One common element in almost every popular treatment of the role of information in the modern economy is a willful disregard for the nature of class. Indeed, the very existence of classes seems to be at odds with the technical requirements of an information-centered economy, where robots and machines do the heavy lifting.

In the future, class will, if anything, become even more important in shaping people's relationship with the labor market. Certainly class seems to be an increasingly important factor in determining access to information. More and more, access to both information and education is becoming privatized. Middle class households can offer their children access to powerful new learning opportunities, such as computers and on line services, which families of poorer children cannot dream of affording (Schiller 1995).

Bites and Bits and Bytes

Reading the hype about the information age, one could almost imagine purveyors of information trucking their products along the information superhighway as if they were so much detergent or canned soup. In fact, as we shall see, information is altogether different from other commodities.

Many people approach the subject of information in a way similar to the way in which they relate to pornography. They are supremely confident that they recognize it when they see it, even if nobody is able to explain exactly what it is. Indeed, since we communicate with information, any definition of information becomes somewhat self-referential.

While I do not pretend to have the definitive word on information, I can say that information is unlike most other commodities. To begin with, unlike, say, soup or detergent, few of us has much need for information as such. For example, thrifty shoppers often scour the papers for coupons to use at the grocery store perhaps to save a few pennies on their detergent or canned soup. Shoppers cannot know in advance what coupons they will find. Even though grocery chains might seem as if they offer discounts for a random set of groceries, shoppers still take the time to clip coupons because most goods at a supermarket have a certain degree of use value in themselves.

Unlike groceries, information, as such, has little value in itself. Few of us would find much benefit in the ability to access streams of random information. Just imagine yourself on a long airline flight sitting next to someone whose idea of a conversation was rattling off random facts, such as the population of Ulan Bator or the molecular weight of cadmium. Mostly, we demand information to allow us to accomplish some specific material objective.

The dictionary definition of information is the communication of knowledge, but the concept of information has expanded to the point that it has become little more than a vague metaphor. Genes now constitute information. Animal cries and human gestures convey information. That sort of information, of course, has always been of vital importance to us. Every creature needs information about how to find food and other basic needs.

What seems to set the information age apart from earlier epochs is the widespread codification of information; that is, general knowledge is worked into a form that simplifies its transfer from one party to another.

Unlike wisdom, information is devoid of any moral or social values. Information is purely operational. For example, a chef might have special knowledge about making a particular dish. She can train another chef to replicate the dish, but her knowledge is not quite information. Once the chef sets her secrets down in the form of a recipe, she transforms knowledge into information. Supposedly, anyone with the appropriate training can read the recipe if it is detailed enough, then put the ingredients together as stated, and recreate the chef's dish.

The recipe is now depersonalized. Once the chef sets it down, her presence is no longer needed by someone with the proper training. This depersonalization and formalization are integral parts of the creation of information.

We shall see that this codification is also associated with specialization. Probably nobody today is capable of learning how to build a nuclear reactor, splice genes, and translate ancient verse. Today, we live in a world of narrow occupational specialization in which specialized equipment is devoted solely to the processing of particular types of information.

In the market societies, we find a more troubling aspect of information: the creation of strong intellectual property rights in information that allows more and more private corporations to profit from the sale of information as a commodity. These intellectual property rights are fast becoming a defining characteristic of our society.

Indeed, a fault line is beginning to run through our society dividing information haves from information have-nots. Our access to information, in turn, is an important determinant of our personal circumstances. It helps us to form our images of ourselves. It signals us about the sort of opportunities that we should pursue. It gives us an entree to good jobs. Information is a major input in the production of what we economists denote as human capital. The processing of information even helps to shape the structure of our brains.

Theoretically, the emerging technologies of the information age could challenge the powers of the great corporation. New modes of communication do have a potential to create alternative institutions to challenge the status quo, but, alas, I do not see any evidence that any such developments represent a substantial threat to the corporate dominance in the advanced capitalist societies.

In this book, we will be more concerned with the social rather than the personal influence of information. Specifically, I will try to address the role of the production of and access to information in the formation of classes. We will see that class is an important element in the demand for information since our circumstances shape our informational needs. A weather report has different meanings for a farmer, a fuel oil speculator, and a vacationer.

Social Factors and the Consumption of Information

The unusual nature of information as a commodity intensifies its role in shaping the modern class structure. Unpacking information is more complex than unpacking detergents or soups. This process generally requires a certain degree of exposure, if not formal training. In a traditional society, young people may participate in as many hours of ceremony as a child might spend in attending classes in our own society. These ceremonies convey the social information needed to allow the society to function.

In our own society, over and above the time we spend in formal schooling, we devote considerable time to training ourselves to use information. For example, most of us have some understanding of the weather maps we see on the television news. These maps would make no sense whatsoever to the uninitiated. Many people absorb sufficient information to gain some understanding of these maps after hours of watching these reports. Over time, an attentive viewer might even pick up a smattering of meteorology.

Even so, mere access to information is insufficient to equip a person for the information age. Most of us require considerable training to allow us to be able to put many kinds of information to use. This training need not be formal, any more than the youth participating in traditional ceremonies and rituals would necessarily see such activities as training.

In fact, play and training often blend into one another. In my youth, when our technologies were primarily mechanical, high school students would often spend much time learning to fix up and to modify automobiles. This hobby prepared many young people for a career working with machines.

Today, electronics has become a major part of our economy. Accordingly, electronic hobbies are becoming more popular and mechanical ones less so. In addition, many careers are beginning to utilize some of the familiarity with a virtual reality that young people experience in their video games. For example, surgeons are more frequently viewing their patients' bodies on computer screens. In some cases, computers control the surgery itself.

Unfortunately, the economics of play works in favor of the well-to-do. Those without a healthy family income are less likely to have the opportunity to play with sophisticated electronics. Forty years ago, you could come by an inexpensive car for relatively little money. A twenty-year-old car at the time might not have had power windows and power steering, but it could have been made to go just as fast as a new one by sticking a newer motor into an older vehicle.

Today, computer technology evolves so fast that a five-year-old computer is hopelessly obsolete. Although the parts are modular—even more so than a car—you cannot mix parts easily from different generations of computers, as you would in an automobile. You might install a faster processor, but then you will need a faster motherboard to handle it. And for many purposes the fast motherboard will require a more modern video card to take advantage of the speed.

The costs of a computer exclude many of the poor from becoming acquainted with the technology. A decent low end computer costs around $1,000. Internet access costs $20 a month and will probably become quite a bit more expensive in the near future.

Forty years ago, a typical parent could instruct a child on mechanics. Today, a child is more likely to be the one to teach the parent about computers.

Where do children learn about these technologies? A child in an affluent neighborhood probably has a number of other people nearby who can offer advice and assistance about computers. A poor child is much less likely to have anybody to whom to turn. In addition, schools in affluent areas are more likely to have computers. As a result, class status is crucially relevant in understanding the role of information within the information economy.

Is the Information Economy Overblown?

Two decades ago, Marc Uri Porat, who later became a co-founder of General Magic Corporation, developed a widely cited estimate of the extent of the information economy. According to Porat, in 1967, 25.1 percent of the U.S. Gross National Product originated with the production, processing, and distribution of information goods and services sold on the market. In addition, the purely informational requirements of planning, coordinating, and managing the rest of the economy consumed another 21.1 percent. In other words, already in the 1960s, Porat estimated that workers whose tasks were predominately informational accounted for almost one-half of the total U.S. economy (Porat 1977, p. 1).

Since Porat's study, the information economy certainly has grown by leaps and bounds. For example, a 1996 study by the Organisation for Economic Cooperation and Development noted that over the past decade for the advanced market economies, the high-technology share of manufacturing production and exports had more than doubled. Knowledge-intensive service sectors, such as education, communication, and information, have been growing even faster (Organisation for European Cooperation and Development, p. 9).

Yet, we should be careful about letting ourselves be carried away by our enthusiasm for the quantitative dimensions of the information economy. To begin with, most researchers find Porat's estimate a bit excessive.

The bulk of the estimates for the size of the information sector in the advanced capitalist countries a decade after Porat's study ran from around 25 percent to 40 percent of the total economy, still a substantial chunk (see Jussawalla 1988, p. 23). Even so, the Organisation for European Cooperation and Development study put the high-technology share of manufacturing production and exports at 20 to 25 percent of the Gross Domestic Product. Using a far more conservative estimate of the information economy, the study concluded that more than 50 percent of Gross Domestic Product in the major OECD economies are now knowledge-based (Organisation for European Cooperation and Development 1996, p. 9).

Of course, here we run into a morass of verbal confusion. To begin with, the very concept of information is amorphous. Does the information in the information economy refer to the information that an industry uses in producing a good or a service as well as the information that the industry delivers to its customers? For example, if a sophisticated computer is used to produce special effects for a mindless film, is it part of the information economy?

In addition, we run into the paradoxical problem that, if the information age were truly upon us, information might turn out to be a shrinking share of the total economy, as Bill Gates suggested when he predicted that information technologies will shrink transaction costs. Unfortunately, reality does not seem to bear out Gates's prediction.

While these new technologies can lower the cost of preparing a bill for a shopper, transaction costs for the economy as a whole have been expanding dramatically and will probably continue to grow. In one study of long-term trends of transaction costs, John Wallis and Douglass North, a Nobel prize-winning economist, analyzed "transactions" industries, such as wholesale and retail trade, banking, insurance, and real estate. They estimate that the transaction component has increased from 25 percent of Gross National Product in 1870 to 45 percent in 1970 (Wallis and North 1986, p. 146 and Table 3.13).

Just consider the explosive growth in financial services. Christopher Niggle notes that the ratio of the book value of financial institutions to the Gross National Product of the United States was 78.4:100 in 1960. In 1970, it was still only 82.9. By 1984, it reached 107.4 (Niggle 1988, p. 585).

Niggle suggests a second ratio to demonstrate the enormous growth of the financial sector: the ratio of financial institutions' assets to the assets of nonfinancial institutions. In 1960, this ratio was 0.957, meaning that the financial and the nonfinancial sectors were about equal. By 1970, the financial sector had overtaken the nonfinancial sector, boosting the ratio to 1.094. By 1983, the dominance of the nonfinancial sector had driven the ratio to 1.202 (Niggle 1988).

Finally, Niggle reports the growing size of the part of the economy known by the acronym FIRE, which stands for Finance, Insurance, and Real Estate. In 1960, the FIRE sector represented 14.3 percent of the Gross Domestic Product of the United States; in 1980, 15.1 percent. The 1983 share of the FIRE sector was 16.4 percent, meaning that within these mere three years the relative importance of the FIRE sector grew by more than it had in the previous 20 years (Niggle 1988).

Nothing better illustrates the dramatic expansion of the FIRE sector than the growth in stock market transactions. In 1960, 766 million shares were traded on the New York Stock Exchange. In 1987, 900 million shares changed hands in the average week. More shares were traded on the lowest volume day in 1987 than in any month in 1960. More shares were traded in the first 15 minutes of October 19 and 20, 1987, than in any week in 1960 (Summers and Summers 1989)

The stock market represents a relatively small share of all financial speculation. Speculators trade many different types of assets. For example, they buy and sell derivative securities, such as stock futures, which provide the rights to buy or sell stocks at a set price at a specified time in the future. Organized markets in such derivative securities did not even exist in 1970. Today, the value of trades in stock futures exceeds that of the trades in stocks themselves. Trade in the New York Stock Exchange averages less than $10 billion per day; government bonds, $25 billion; daily trade in foreign exchange averages more than $25 billion. Trade in index options equals that of stock futures (Summers and Summers 1989).

The shrinking cost of information processing, to which Gates turned our attention, has been an essential element that has allowed the FIRE sector of the economy to expand at the expense of the production of real goods. The continued growth of the FIRE sector stands in sharp contrast to Gates's vision of disappearing transaction costs.

The FIRE sector has also seriously damaged the quality of our lives. With their growing access to information, financial markets can now micromanage firms whose shares trade on the exchange. They have pressured firms to downsize and to move jobs abroad. In terms of the creation of an information economy, financial markets are major barriers. They punish firms whose actions do not lead to immediate profits, thereby pressuring firms to cut back on the research and development expenses that could possibly help us to realize the promise of the information age.

The misguided faith that we could somehow build a vibrant economy on the basis of a purely informational economy has made people more accepting of the destructive downsizing of our manufacturing economy. A viable informational economy requires that the processing of information be linked with traditional manufacturing or agricultural activities (Castells 1996, p. 211; Perelman 1991, pp. 131-5).

Information Quantity or Information Quality?

Kenneth Arrow, a Nobel laureate in economics, once proposed that "[T]he meaning of information is precisely a reduction in uncertainty" (Arrow 1979, p. 306), but he did not adequately distinguish between the value to an individual and the value to society. By Arrow's standard, the recent surge in corporate power has allowed the giant corporations to shift risk and uncertainty from their balance sheet onto the rest of society. As a result, for the typical person today, uncertainty is probably at an all-time high. We are uncertain about our jobs, our health care, our pensions, and our communities.

In addition, our discussion of the FIRE sector indicates why much of the information associated with the information economy is of little or even no value for society as a whole. Other activities, say market research, which we might normally be tempted to count as information producing, should actually also be excluded according to Arrow's standard when we consider society as a whole. At best, we might charitably call such information, "local information." While this information may reduce uncertainty for a particular firm, it may also create more uncertainty for the competitors of that same firm.

Of course, estimating the real value of information is admittedly a subjective exercise. So, let us shift our attention to a different type of information—weather information—before we return to our discussion of the FIRE sector. One study estimates that perfect weather information in the United States would be worth $145 million (Adams et al. 1995, p. 10). Yet, the private weather forecasting industry alone has revenue approaching $200 million a year (Feder 1996), considerably more than the $145 million estimate of the benefits of perfect weather forecasts.

Just who subscribes to such services? Should we be surprised to find our old friends from the FIRE sector? All major Wall Street brokerage houses have their own weather departments. Each one tries to get the best weather information so that it can get an edge on others in speculating in agricultural commodities or fuel oil. While accurate private weather forecasts might be profitable for the individual speculator, the public as a whole does not gain much from the expertise of these private meteorologists.

Other so-called informational activities are probably even counterproductive. For example, Porat's estimate of the information sector mistakenly includes advertising and marketing activities. Perhaps I am unique, but I have never felt particularly grateful when a telemarketer interrupted me to convey some vital "information."

Rather than provide information, professionals design much advertising to do nothing more than to delude and to confuse people in order to get an edge on their competitors without serving consumers' needs in any way. True, some advertising is "constructive," but surely most is merely "combative," having nothing to do with conveying information (see Marshall 1923, pp. 304-7). In fact, we could do better treating such activities as disinformation.

We must recognize that advertising imposes other costs by cluttering up our environment. When we calculate our Gross Domestic Product, we justifiably count the product of industries that beautify our surroundings as making a positive contribution to our lives. The same logic would suggest that we count the damage that advertising does to our environment as a negative contribution.

Besides its ever-increasing intrusiveness and overall unpleasantness, advertising desensitizes us to our surroundings. We can also regard at least some of this junk advertising as disinformation in another sense, since it obscures valuable clues that might otherwise give us valuable information about our environment.

Finally, when advertisers exercise their considerable sway in the media, they degrade our access to important information. For example, our magazines are far more enthusiastic about printing pictures displaying the advantages of smoking a particular brand of cigarettes than in discussing the health effects of cigarettes, lest that information displease a major source of advertising revenue. We should include this cost as part of the ledger on advertising, under the general subheading of disinformation.

We can get some indication of the relative importance of information and disinformation by noting that the 150,000 public relations practitioners in the United States outnumber the country's 130,000 reporters (Dowie 1995). Of course, these numbers must be taken with a grain of salt. A growing number of reporters are indistinguishable from the public relations industry. One study found that 38 percent of journalists get at least half their story ideas from public relations sources (Walker 1991).

Virtually all 150 newspaper editors in a 1992 study by Lawrence C. Soley, Colnik Professor of Communication at Marquette University, and Robert L. Craig, a former Marquette professor now teaching at the University of Ulster, acknowledged interference by advertisers. According to the survey, 93 percent of editors said advertisers tried to influence the content of their newspaper articles. Seventy-one percent of editors said advertisers tried to kill certain stories outright. Thirty-seven percent of editors were honest enough to admit that they actually had succumbed to this advertiser pressure. More than half (55.1 percent) said there was pressure from within their own newspapers to write or tailor news stories to please advertisers (Kerwin 1993, p. 28).

A recent front-page story in the *Wall Street Journal* reported that large advertisers now commonly require prior notification of any story that might reflect poorly on the advertisers' product either by putting its product in a bad light or by offending the readers' sensibilities in any way (Knecht 1997).

The public relations industry considers this state of affairs to be healthy. For example, Edward Bernays, double nephew of Sigmund Freud and often described as the "father of public relations," began his book, *Propaganda,* by stating:

> The conscious and intelligent manipulation of the organized habits and opinions of the masses is an important element in democratic society. Those who manipulate this unseen mechanism of society constitute an invisible government that is the true ruling power of our country. (Bernays 1928, p. 9)

Bernays proudly called his scientific technique of opinion molding "the engineering of consent," which is the title of a book that he edited. Based on the lack of protest against the techniques, public relations, he concluded that "We have voluntarily agreed to let an invisible government sift the data and high-spot the outstanding issues" (Bernays 1928, p. 11).

Curiously, Bernays's understanding of public relations dovetails with Porat's definition of information. For Porat, "Information is data that have been organized and communicated" (Porat 1977, p. 2). Who then will have the power and the opportunity to organize and communicate data in a class society?

A Different Information Economy

To some extent, the whole notion of an information economy may be an exercise in hubris. We take great pride in our increasing command of information without recognizing that we do not necessarily distinguish ourselves from other societies by our more sophisticated use of information. Instead, other societies merely use different types of information. In a sense, we might even propose that the real novelty of the information economy is not the informational content of our society at all but merely our consciousness of the informational aspects of work. While we know more about computers, astrophysics, and the stock market than our forbearers, we know less about other things.

For example, earlier students were often familiar with the classics of Latin and Greek literature. In fact, even seemingly primitive peoples had a deep understanding of the biology of their surroundings. For example, according to Edgar Anderson, during the last 5,000 years modern society has not domesticated a single plant that primitive cultures had not already used. He points out that traditional cultures had already managed to discover all five natural sources of caffeine: coffee, tea, the cola plant, cacao, yerba mate, and its relatives (Anderson 1952, pp. 132-3).

In many respects, contemporary biologists still lag behind traditional societies in understanding the biological properties of the flora that surround them. Even today, approximately 25 percent of all pharmaceuticals contain some natural product (Day and Frisvold 1992). So-called primitive people were aware of many if not most of these properties.

Scientists are just beginning to understand the biological rationale for primitive agricultural practices (Gupta 1990). Admittedly, much of the non-medicinal, indigenous knowledge is not easily transferred to the core market economy. Much of this information is valuable only within the context of indigenous traditions and customs (Agrawal 1995, pp. 431-2). This condition is not unique to indigenous traditions. In fact, the value of much of our own modern technology, as well as a considerable portion of the mass of our accumulated information, is also contingent upon the existing structure of society.

Let me refer to a rather crude example. Until widespread public protests caused them to be outlawed, many farm workers in California used short-handled hoes. These implements are no more efficient than the more familiar hoe. Moreover, they took a terrible toll on the backs of farm workers who were forced to hold their spines in unnatural positions for extended periods of time, placing a great strain on the back.

The real advantage of the short handle was not technical at all, but informational. Because of the inadequate length of the handle, the short-handled hoe forces the worker to stoop in an uncomfortable position. This attribute of the hoe allowed the overseer to see when workers relaxed, since they would naturally stand erect to relieve the pressure on their backs whenever possible.

Farmers appreciated this particular tool because of its ability to convey information to those who managed the field crews. This information was quite economical for the farmers. Unfortunately, it was costly to the farm workers. As would be expected, the continual bending frequently caused serious back injuries. Nonetheless, farming interests fought vigorously to continue the use of the short-handled hoe, often proclaiming that they were acting in the best interest of their employees (see Perelman 1977).

Porat and the other accountants of the information economy would not include the short-handled hoe as an informational device along with computers and other information processing equipment. Nonetheless, the crude, short-handled hoe served to monitor workers just as surely as the sophisticated electronic appliances in use in the advanced workplaces of our modern information economy.

Notice that, just as in the case of some of the "primitive" information discussed above, the sort of information associated with the short-handled hoe is useful only in a particular type of society—one in which the lives of those who do the work have little value. Again, we see a close relationship between the way a society constructs its information and the underlying class structure.

Ernesto Galarza, one of the truly great advocates of the rights of agricultural labor, offered valuable insight into another sort of informational processing associated with agricultural fieldwork, a class of labor thought to be among the most unskilled known to modern society:

> Field labor was a blur in which the details of field harvesting and the skills it required went unrecognized. To pick ripe honeydew requires a trained eye for the bloom of tinted cream, a sensitive touch for the waxy feeling of the rind, and a discriminating nose for the faint aroma of ripeness. In the asparagus fields, the expertness of the Filipino cutters was obvious to all but those who hired them. (Galarza 1977, pp. 29 and 366)

We do not typically think of such activities as informational. Of course, virtually all life involves the processing of information. A bird on a migratory flight or a honeybee returning to its nest is processing information. Even single celled organisms respond to information about their environment.

We generally mean something else by information. Even if we restrict ourselves to considering only data processing as informational, we still discover informational activities in unexpected corners of our economy.

As we noted earlier, we generally restrict our understanding of the information economy to those parts of the economy in which a person is more or less exclusively processing symbols rather than using knowledge and experience in the course of useful physical work on material objects. Consider how a symbolic analyst would function in the agricultural fields.

Suppose we would divide up fieldwork into two jobs. One worker goes into the fields and inspects the produce and then writes a report on each individual melon. The second worker reads the report in order to know which melons to retrieve. Suddenly, fieldwork would seem very informational. The fact that the field workers rely on their tacit knowledge, which remains internal to them, makes their job seem more primitive and certainly less informational.

Those who have studied the development of agricultural technology know full well that if fieldwork did not require considerable human decision making, it would have been mechanized long ago. The tomato is a perfect example. Many tomatoes are now bred to be hard enough so that they ripen slowly. As a result, freshness is not a concern when picking them. Machines now pick these tomatoes since the new breed of tomatoes has made the worker's judgment inconsequential. As anyone who has eaten these tomatoes knows, something is lost in the process. In doing away with the judgment of the workers, the delicious taste of a fresh tomato also vanishes.

Many people do not expect to find informational work in the fields among people whom they do not respect. They see the fieldworker as an ignorant soul, perhaps even unable to speak our language properly. In general, we tend to associate informational work with people who have enjoyed higher education and who wear expensive clothing. Again, a sense of class seems to color the way we understand informational work.

The way that we classify informational workers is changing for two reasons. First, one of the hallmarks of the information economy is an ever-expanding conception of information. With the transformation of images and voice, as well as data, to digital form, alongside the more general commodification of cultural life, the distinction between data proper and, say, a movie, becomes blurred within the newly invented category of intellectual property. The vast flow of executives from the fast food and beverage industry to the management suites of the computer industry is symbolic of this broadening of the nature of information.

2

Classes and the Information Revolution

Information Economy and the Organization of Work

We overstate the information economy for still another reason. A good portion of the apparent growth of the information sector is nothing more than an illusion, arising out of changes in the organizational structure of the economy.

With increasing specialization of labor, we see more and more occupations in which a worker's predominate activity is information processing, even though the total quantity of information processing might not change. Jagdish Bhagwati has made much of the effect of this specialization in his analysis of services, where he writes of the "continuous process during which services splinter off from goods and goods, in turn, splinter off from services" (Bhagwati 1984, p. 134).

Let us see why this appearance of suboccupations does not necessarily represent an increase in the informational content of the economy. Today, instead of employing a carpenter to build a house, we first employ an architect to design it. Architects are part of the information sector, but carpenters have never been treated that way, even when they routinely performed design work in the course of building houses. The split between carpenters and architects parallels the imaginary bifurcation of agricultural fieldwork that I discussed earlier.

True, the increase in the number of architects is not altogether arbitrary, as was the hypothetical case of the farm workers. More complex buildings and more stringent building codes do require an increase in the informational content of the construction industry. Even so, if we count the expanded work of the architects and designers as part of the increase in the information economy, then we must also take into account the declining informational activities of the carpenters.

I do not mean that the carpenters are not engaged in informational work anymore. They certainly are. I only want to convey that the nature of the modern construction industry limits the discretion and autonomy of the carpenter by moving a considerable part of the design work from the carpenter to the architect and other specialists.

I do not pretend, of course, that the growth of the information economy is merely a matter of a redefinition of information. Obviously, the informational content of our economy has expanded enormously, measured in terms of the flow of data. This discussion is merely meant to indicate that the growth of the information economy has not been as dramatic as we might otherwise imagine.

This correction might help us to avoid losing sight of the fact that this reallocation of the informational responsibilities is closely related to the changing class structure of the economy. The imagery of an information economy conveys a picture of comfortable white-collar workers in an air-conditioned office devoting their working day to the processing of information. This perspective lulls us into overlooking the unfortunate workers, say, in a semiconductor factory bathed in toxic fumes or at a sterile bank of computer terminals while their repetitive work causes them to develop carpal tunnel syndrome.

Those who promote the utopian imagery of an information age also forget the masses of service workers who provide for the comfort of the information elite. We conveniently leave out of their vision of the information age the uncomfortable fact that:

> High-income gentrification [is inseparable from] . . . the increase in the numbers of expensive restaurants, luxury housing, luxury hotels, gourmet shops, boutiques, French hand laundries, and special cleaners that ornament the new urban landscape [which creates a] continuing need for low-wage industrial services, even in such sectors as finance and specialized services. (Sassen 1991, p. 9)

So class relationships continue in the information age, albeit in a muddled way.

The Cruel Hoax of an Information Economy

In warding off excessive enthusiasm about the information economy, we should not overreact by pretending that modern informational technologies are no different than the technologies that preceded them. Just as railroads provided benefits to society that canals could not provide, so too do computers and other informational technologies offer the promise of enormous advances in the quality of our lives. However, we are doing little to ready ourselves for anything like an information age.

If we were seriously preparing ourselves for an information economy, we would be devoting more and more resources to education. Unfortunately, other priorities rank far higher than education in our society. In California, where I live, the state once had a generous educational system. Today, state spending on prisons has now surpassed state funding of higher education.

Universities have met the challenge of declining funds by decreasing the quality of education, lowering wages and salaries of their employees (except for their highly placed administrators) and by increasing tuition costs. More and more, college and university students must work longer hours to earn enough money to pay for rising tuition and other costs of their education, cutting into their ability to learn. Too many of their teachers are harried part timers who have to cobble together two or three teaching jobs just to make ends meet.

Although the fiscal crisis of higher education is serious, the situation in primary and secondary education is catastrophic. Rather than raising the taxes necessary for an adequate educational system, today, cost cutting in education is all the rage.

We can never know exactly what fuels the conservative attack on education in the United States, but a number of forces seem to have come together. Religious fundamentalists are among the most active foot soldiers in the war on public education. Many sincerely believe that the state has no place in educating children, especially when scientific principles conflict with strongly held dogma. Accordingly, they hold that parents or the church are the appropriate sources of instruction.

Although the fundamentalists' activities are counterproductive to the needs of an educated workforce, they have been amazingly effective in a larger movement to curtail the ability of the government to control corporate behavior or to raise taxes. Since, with increasing globalization, corporations have less need for educated workers at home, the benefits of lower taxes and deregulation, and the detruction of education must seem like a small price to pay. In addition, with widespread downsizing, the corporations already enjoy an ample supply of educated workers. Finally, a few corporations now see privatized education as an entirely new profit center.

Illustrative of the changing status of education, we might note that three decades ago, even Milton Friedman, the doyen of conservative economists argued in favor of generous government support of education, albeit through vouchers, because of the importance of an educated populace (Friedman 1962, Chapter 6). Today, dogmatic conservatives still advocate vouchers, but more as a way of cutting taxes or opening up business opportunities for profit-oriented educational businesses.

Today, public education is caught in a downward spiral. Pressing social problems make the work of public education more difficult. The inability to solve these problems leads to less financial support, which makes the schools less able to deliver.

The effect of the conservative tide is obvious in education, especially in the case of poor children, who never got the same educational opportunities as children from more affluent families (Carnoy 1994, pp. 134-5). For example, in 1989, Chicago spent some $5,500 for each student in its secondary schools, compared to some $8,500 to $9,000 for each high school student in the highest-spending suburbs to the north. In New York from 1986-1987, funding per student was $11,300 in the upper-middle-class Long Island suburbs of Manhasset, Jericho, and Great Neck; $6,400 in the largely working-class suburb of Mount Vernon; and $5,600 in the high-minority New York City public schools. Three years later, the figures were $15,000, $9,000, and $7,300 respectively. Although the proportionate change was equal, the absolute change favored the already rich districts (Kozol 1991, pp. 54 and 237).

Suburban schools are generally newer, while inner city and, to a lesser extent, rural schools are often in a state of disrepair. As a result, the poorer school districts face higher costs of operating their physical plant than the more affluent suburban schools. For example, a General Accounting Office report to Congress noted that "one third of the nation's 80,000 public schools are in such poor repair that the fourteen million children who attend them are being housed in unsuitable or unsafe conditions" (Schiller 1995, p. 76; citing Honan 1995). Jonathan Kozol described a rather extreme instance: the Martin Luther King Junior High School in East St. Louis, Illinois, where sewage repeatedly backed up into the school, including the food preparation area (Kozol 1991, p. 21).

Not surprisingly, dropout rates are abominable. More than 20 percent of the nation's students drop out before completing high school. In many inner cities, the number is as high as 50 percent (Commission on the Skills of the American Workforce 1990, p. 47).

In the midst of grinding poverty, many students who do stay in school need to find employment, detracting from their education. A North Carolina study of high school juniors found that half work, with two-thirds of those working holding jobs of twenty hours or more a week. Scott D.

Thomson, director of a national school principals' association, lamented that in "other nations school is considered too important for students to work" (Jacoby 1994, p. 19).

While conservatives comfort themselves by insisting that money is more or less irrelevant to economic outcomes, economic studies find that a 10 percent increase in educational expenditures per student is associated with a 1 to 2 percent increase in the students' eventual annual earnings (Card and Krueger 1996). Sadly, they are far off the mark.

While society teaches the children that it does not care about them, society is shocked that many children display a similar disregard for society. We are appalled to learn that, in 1992, teachers and authorities confiscated almost 400 guns in Los Angeles schools alone, including 33 in elementary school (Jacoby 1994, p. 196).

Even from a narrow fiscal standpoint, our neglect of the schools is an expensive proposition. According to the New York City Department of Corrections, 90 percent of the male inmates of the city's prison are the former dropouts of the city's public schools. Incarceration of each inmate, the department notes, costs the city nearly $60,000 every year (Kozol 1991, p. 118).

Of course, we cannot blame too much on inadequate educational funding. In part, the way we finance different people's education is merely a reflection of a wider set of social forces that treats members of different classes differently. However, we certainly do a better job in our society of preparing our underprivileged youth for prison than for productive and meaningful employment.

Perhaps we should expect this outcome. After all, despite all the grand rhetoric about the information age, we find more and more of our jobs outside of what we might consider to be the information economy. The proportion of workers earning poverty level wages continues to increase (Mishel and Bernstein 1994, pp. 124-6). Sadly, most new jobs in the United States, for example, are in the low wage service industry where the informational requirements are minimal. For example, the occupations that the United States Bureau of Labor Statistics expects to show the most absolute growth are, in descending order, cashiers; janitors and cleaners, including maids and housekeeping cleaners; retail sales persons; and waiters and waitresses (Silvestri 1996).

The future promises little improvement. More than 70 percent of the jobs in the United States will not require a college education by the year 2000. More than one-third will require little more than an eighth grade education (Commission on the Skills of the American Workforce 1990, pp. 26-7).

Even those with college educations are not immune to the downward spiral. According to a report from the Collegiate Employment Research Institute at Michigan State University, based on a survey of over 500 Organizations that recruit college graduates:

> There are not enough jobs for the number of college graduates produced. . . . More people are getting college degrees, but the educational level required for adequate job performance is not rising as rapidly as the number of new college graduates produced by colleges and universities throughout the country. . . . Even with a college degree, there is no guarantee of a job or career requiring a college degree, or any job for that matter. (cited in Mandel 1996, p. 120)

Economists often tell us that lack of skills is responsible for the ever more unequal distribution of income. The poor, we are told, just do not have the capacity to compete in a high tech economy. If the schools do not prepare children for this environment, who will? Can we expect their equally unprepared parents to provide them with the proper job training? And even those with good training find themselves unable to apply their skills in the job market.

In the next section, we will discuss the plight of those with graduate degrees. So, for the majority of our population the promise of an information economy remains a cruel hoax.

Squandering Educational Resources

Equally appalling is our failure to put to good use the skills of those people who earn graduate degrees in science. Throughout the Cold War, the military-industrial complex was the primary employer of scientists. For more than a decade now, our universities have been educating far more people with doctorates in science than our economy can accommodate— at least as the economy is presently structured.

For example, in December 1995, the Joint Policy Board for Mathematics announced an unemployment rate of 14.7 percent for the 1,226 doctorates awarded in 1995, the highest ever reported. An additional 4.2 percent were in part-time jobs, and of those employed in academe, 61 percent were not in positions eligible for tenure (Magner 1996).

By 1987, 60.5 percent of employed Ph.D.'s who had earned their degrees in the physical sciences between 1980 and 1982 were working in business or industry (Stephan and Levin 1992, p. 97). Many of these jobs have little promise of producing any social benefit. For example, a steady stream of Ph.D. physicists find work on Wall Street calculating strategies for investing in derivatives and other financial instruments (Mukerjee 1994). Still more, even if they do find work related to their education, they will find their skills severely underemployed. Employment prospects are substantially worse for other fields whose expertise appears to be less applicable to the immediate commercial needs of an information economy.

Manpower Inc., the nation's largest temporary agency, plans to provide holders of advanced physics degrees to corporate clients, mostly in the computer and electronics industries. Though few of the temps would be working directly as physicists, Manpower hopes to place them in related jobs, such as developing new computer chips or writing software programs. Mitchell Fromstein, Manpower's chairman, said that if Manpower's physicists catch on, "we'll offer chemistry Ph.D.'s next." "Times have changed for physicists: There are jobs, but physicists have to be more flexible than they were in the past," said John Rigden, director of physics programs at American Institute of Physics (Zachary 1996).

The majority of scientists with new Ph.D.'s who obtain jobs in an academic setting must settle for temporary positions called "postdoctorals" that allow the graduate time to publish and gain other forms of distinction. Supposedly, the postdoctoral appointment will allow the graduate a better chance to obtain a permanent position, but the growing number of postdoctoral personnel suggests great competition for more secure employment (Stephan 1996, p. 1214).

Today scientists who are unable to get permanent jobs just move from one postdoctoral position to another. In the physical sciences, for example, in the late 1970s as many as one out of every ten Ph.D.'s who had been out for four years had a postdoctorate; by the late 1980s, this number had grown to one out of every eight (Stephan and Levin 1992, p. 96).

Yes, times are changing. As government continues to cut the funds for higher education, the squeeze on scientists will no doubt become even worse, further discouraging young people from seeking careers in science in the future. As this process continues, the average age of university scientists continues to grow (Stephan and Levin 1992, p. 6). This aging of the scientific community represents another serious dimension to the crisis since most of the breakthroughs in science come from the young (Stephan and Levin 1992, Chapters 3 and 4).

What then can we say about the future of our information economy, which is unable to find any use for the skills of those most prepared to further our informational capacity?

The Real Information Revolution

What is the information revolution? Certainly, it is not what I would hope an information revolution would be—a transformation of society in which access to information would empower people to lead their lives to the fullest. Within such a revolution, information would relieve people of boring, dangerous, and monotonous work. It would provide more leisure. It would allow people to explore their own potential. We see none of this for the great masses of people.

The real information revolution that is taking place is very different indeed. I can identify two factors that make our relationship to information revolutionary.

To begin with, we now treat information as private property. This approach to information is indeed revolutionary. In many earlier societies, information was probably a shared resource. Somehow, small groups within society came into exclusive possession of information. This information could be real or imaginary, as, say, in the power of witchcraft. In either case, it gave one group power over another.

For example, members of the ancient Egyptian priesthood developed information about the timing of the flooding of the Nile. This information was of vital importance for farmers who needed to coordinate the agricultural cycle with the state of the river. As in Arrow's conception of information, this knowledge reduced uncertainty.

In return for access to the priests' information about the flooding, their followers sacrificed a measure of control over their lives by following the teachings of the priests and in giving the priests some material support. In the process, the priests achieved a position of substantial control within their society, whether they used their powers at the behest of the pharaoh or in their own right.

The ancient Egyptian priests were unlikely to have demanded a direct payment for their information. After all, such information was sacred. Certainly, they benefitted from their information, but something subtler than a purchase and sale was at work.

With the development of Western civilization, scientists treated science as a common resource, except in the relatively rare cases in which a state would hire a scientist for some military project. Scientists were happy to share their work with the larger community of scientists. More often than not their reward was the acclaim they won for their achievements.

We could think of a patent as a break with this tradition, although patents themselves also have a long tradition. As early as the fourteenth century, some Italian states began to issue patents to encourage inventors to develop useful technology (Merges 1995). More often than not, patents gave only temporary and insecure rights. In addition, they were rarely bought and sold.

The idea of intellectual property is a truly revolutionary concept. We will see that it has profound consequences for the future of science and technology.

The second revolutionary factor of the information age is the ability to collect and organize information into databases that reach into the innermost recesses of our lives. This phenomenon has enormous consequences that do not bode well for the future.

The databases typically are the property of giant corporations or the government. Corporations seek to amass this information as a source of power and wealth rather than human betterment. They may want to deploy this information directly or to market it in the form of a commodity.

Private individuals, as a rule, do not have direct access to these great databases. The owner may provide bits and pieces of these databases for public consumption, but the database generally remains internal to the government or the corporation. If a great database is for sale, its price puts it well beyond the means of the ordinary citizen.

The more information a corporation has, the more information it can collect. For example, sophisticated technologies also permit those who offer information to extract sacrifices of information from those who seek it.

Just think of how the World Wide Web works. Corporations develop intriguing web pages promising information or pure entertainment. Like Venus's-flytraps these pages lure unsuspecting Web surfers to provide information themselves. Some firms merely collect the address of those who alight on their Web pages. Others entice visitors to supply more personal information.

In effect, those who seek to acquire this information may unwittingly give up a degree of control to those who supply the information, just as surely as the ancient Egyptians did. In this sense, these databases take on lives of their own.

In addition, as we already noted, the information suppliers provide can convey misinformation or even propaganda to the unsuspecting. You may recall the attempt during the 1950s to perfect methods of subliminal advertising (Packard 1981) or the use of product placement in contemporary films and television.

While Arrow's idea that information serves to reduce uncertainty has some merit, I suggest that we would do better to think of the overarching purpose of acquiring information as control. Information can be used to control things or processes. The object of control may be other people or even ourselves, since we use information to alter our own moods or even to foster the development of our brains.

Given the close relationship between information and control, we have good reason to be troubled. I am convinced that the real revolution in the information age at hand is twofold. First, more and more we are treating information as private property. Second, we are standing by while the giant corporations and the government are developing a virtual monopoly of information.

Of course, just turning information over to those who have been denied the training to use it would do them little good. We need only recall Speaker of the U.S. House of Representatives Newt Gingrich's laughable proposal that we should end poverty by providing laptop computers to the unfortunate who find themselves homeless or on welfare. Certainly many of these people could benefit from acquiring computer skills, but hardware alone is woefully insufficient. Most people who are competent with computers have previously benefitted by associating with others who already had valuable knowledge of the technology.

What About Classes?

What about classes in the information economy? In an earlier age, class analysis was a relatively easy proposition. We had readily identifiable workers and capitalists. Supposedly, even the untrained eye could recognize workers by their costumes—for example, people commonly spoke of white-, blue-, or pink-collar workers. A few professionals complicated the picture, but they never made class analysts feel terribly uncomfortable.

Today, things are much more difficult. More and more, even skilled professionals—doctors, accountants, and lawyers—find themselves slipping into the abyss of contingent, proletarianized labor (see Kletke, Emmons, and Ellis 1996). At the same time, other wage workers with specialized skills enjoy incomes achieved only by a select elite of the capitalists. For example, the net worth of an elite athlete may rival or even exceed that of his employer.

The world of the capitalists is just as confusing. For example, the practice of franchising creates an entirely new class of capitalists, whose status within the overall organization may resemble that of a worker, albeit a supervisory worker.

In the face of such complexity, conservative forces insist that any consideration of classes is counterproductive. In fact, this denial of class is most untimely. True, individuals are becoming more atomized; however, this phenomenon is part of a much larger process. While the modern in-

formation economy weakens the power of isolated individuals to understand, let alone assert their class interests, the same forces have been rein-
forcing the power of the ruling classes to wield class power.

With this hardening of the class system, more and more wealth and income flows to the upper classes, leading to a scandalous distribution of
income within the United States. After becoming more egalitarian during
the 1930s through the mid-1960s, a reversal in the distribution of income
began in the late 1960s. It continued through the 1970s. By the 1980s, the
process quickened. For example, between 1979 and 1989, the economy
enjoyed healthy growth, but the top one percent of households got 70
percent of all of the increase in income (Krugman 1992, p. 23).

The change in the distribution of wealth was even more extreme than
the distribution of income. Between 1983 and 1989, the share of the top
one percent of wealth holders rose by five percentage points. Almost all
the increases in wealth accrued to the top 20 percent. The wealth of the
bottom 40 percent showed an absolute decline despite strong economic
growth (Wolff 1995, p. 7).

Despite the harsh economic realities, almost nobody broached the
question of class during this period. Poor whites were taught to blame
their problems on the government or affirmative action, while people of
color were demonized. Discussion of class remained a political taboo.

In this environment for many affluent members of modern society, the
mirage of a classless information age appears to be at hand. They have
computers, on-line services, the Internet, cable modems, and the like. Certainly, one of the joys of our virtual reality is the privilege of choosing the
world we want to see.

Within the context of the material reality, the affluent remain a distinct mi-
nority. Many of our beloved computer components come from the same sort
of places as those that produce our running shoes—communities where poor,
overworked people barely eke out a living in unwholesome sweatshops.

I do not intend to address the injustices of the class system in this
book. My concern here will be to show that the existence of classes conflicts with the requirements of an information age. In other words, so long
as we permit the existing class structure to remain in place, we will never
be able to enjoy the promise of an information age.

Social Fragmentation in the Information Age

Within the harsh reality of our modern economy, we continue to drift further away from the sort of organization of society that could allow us to

take advantage of the liberating potential of the accumulated knowledge of the world. Class still exerts a profound influence on the way people's self images develop. Self-image, in turn, exerts a profound influence on the way people develop their job skills.

One need only step inside a public school. Within a few seconds, the casual observer can fairly accurately determine the class origins of the bulk of the students. The relatively few people who do manage to rise above their class origins obscure the class nature of our society, thus making it more resistant to challenge.

The rhetoric of individualism further cloaks the madness of this class-ridden society. For example, Margaret Thatcher boldly insisted in a London publication, *Woman's Own,* "There is no such thing as society: there are individual men and women, and there are families" (31 October 1987).

Thatcher's words contain a grain of truth. We are indeed experiencing more individualism of a sort, but this individualism does not promise meaningful freedom as much as isolation. For example, in the modern information age, face to face communication is giving way to electronic mail. I realize that electronic mail can give rise to new types of communities and that this medium of communication may be seen, in a sense, as more direct than traditional mail, which had once entailed lengthy delays.

I admit that electronic mail can potentially facilitate a sense of community. Yes, in some cases, massive deluges of electronic mail have on occasion been mobilized, but since this form of mobilization requires virtually no commitment, the powers that be have little reason to take it as seriously as they would huge numbers of human beings gathered together in a protest demonstration.

While the modern information age may make us feel like isolated individuals, the same forces intensify the class nature of our actual conditions. Let us take a simple example. Today, a firm may employ a multitude of telecommuters, people who work at home while connected with work through computers. None of these workers need know one another since each works at home. This isolation may give some of the workers a degree of independence, in the sense that they can work in familiar surroundings, perhaps even at flexible times. This same isolation, however, reinforces the strength of the employing firm relative to each individual worker, just as massing of workers together in large-scale work sites tended to strengthen working class power in an earlier era.

Observers from the early days of capitalism clearly recognized the importance of this phenomenon. For example, Josiah Tucker, a contemporary of Adam Smith, noted that, in the West Country where a more advanced factory system existed:

The Motives to Industry, Frugality and Sobriety are all subverted to this one consideration viz. that they shall always be chained to the same Oar (the Clothier), and never be but Journeymen. . . . Is it little wonder that the trade in Yorkshire should flourish, or the trade in Somersetshire, Wiltshire, and Gloucestershire be found declining every day?

One Person, with a great Stock and large Credit, buys the Wool, pays for the Spinning, Weaving, Milling, Dying, Shearing, Dressing, etc., etc. That is, he is the Master of the whole Manufacture from first to last, and perhaps employs a Thousand persons under him. This is the Clothier whom all the Rest are to look upon as their Paymaster. But will they not also sometimes look upon him as their Tyrant? And as great Numbers of them work together in the same Shop, will they not have it more in their Power to vitiate and corrupt each other, to cabal and associate against their Masters, and to break out in Mobs and Riots upon every little Occasion?. . . Besides, as the Master is placed so high above the Condition of the Journeymen, both their Conditions approach much nearer that of Planter and Slave in our American Colonies, than might be expected in such a Country as England; and the Vices and Tempers belonging to each Condition are of the same Kind, only in inferior Degree. The Master, for Example, however well-disposed in himself, is naturally tempted by his Situation to be proud and overbearing, to consider his People as the Scum of the earth, whom he has a Right to squeeze whenever he can; because they ought to be kept low, and not to rise up in Compensation with their Superiors. The journeymen, on the contrary, are equally tempted by their Situation, to envy the high Station, and superior Fortunes of their Masters; and to envy them the more, in Proportion as they find themselves deprived of the Hopes of advancing themselves to the same Degree by any Stretch of Industry, or superior Skill. Hence their Self-love takes a wrong Turn, destructive to themselves, and others. They think it no Crime to get as much Wages, and to do as little for it as they possibly can, to lie and cheat, and do any other bad Thing; provided it is only against their Master, whom they look upon as their common Enemy, with whom no Faith is kept. . . . [T]heir only Happiness is to get Drunk, and to make Life pass away with as little Thought as possible. (Tucker, pp. 37-9)

A similar interest in fragmenting the working class led employers to disperse manufacturing from the central city throughout the early twentieth century (Gordon 1978). The readiness of the federal government to subsidize suburban development in the period after World War II may well reflect an effort at breaking up remnants of the strong, working class communities that had developed in urban areas near the remaining major factories.

Presently, relatively few people enjoy significant access to any of the levers of society. Ultimately, information technologies might allow people around the world to form a global community that could stand up to the powerful corporations that now wield these technologies. So far I know of no evidence that such a possibility is actually taking place. Rather than enjoying the formation of a global village, we are witnessing what some have appropriately called global pillage (Brecher and Costello 1994).

3

Information and the Control of the Labor Process

Popular accounts of our emerging information economy rarely treat information as a means of control. This silence does not constitute evidence that information and control are unrelated. In fact, economists have only recently recognized the importance of information in production. Typically, economists had represented the production process as a mechanistic recipe in which the employer mixed together a predetermined formula consisting of specified amounts of labor and capital.

Ideology played a part in this approach. In the eighteenth and nineteenth centuries, many workers refused to accept the idea that employers deserved great wealth by virtue of their ownership of capital. They contended that only labor produced wealth and that labor deserved the wealth that it produced.

By portraying workers as unthinking objects, economists downplayed labor's claim to a larger share of the wealth that it produced. Our languages reinforced this vision. In the Germanic languages, we refer to labor as hands; in the Romance languages, as arms.

Over and above ideological considerations, the question of information was vital at the time for very practical reasons. Prior to the rise of the giant corporation, workers possessed the bulk of information about production techniques. Their information was not intellectual property in the sense that they had any exclusive legal right to that information. The information was theirs only because they consciously kept this information a secret from outsiders.

These workers clearly understood the value of this secrecy. Sometimes, they even shrouded the "mysteries" of their trades in secret rituals, faintly echoed today in the Masonic rites that supposedly came out of ancient Egypt. These traditions may represent a link between the private knowledge of the early priesthoods and that of the skilled craft workers.

Well into the late nineteenth century, managers in many industries remained ignorant about the labor process. This situation could not last for long. The German philosopher G.W.F. Hegel understood this phenomenon when he wrote about the reversal of power in slave society. He noted perceptively that when slaves were the sole masters of the production process, masters became superficial dependents of the slaves (Hegel 1807, p. 118).

Management hoped to be able to gain enough control over the production process that they could treat their employees more like interchangeable parts. If a few workers dared to demand more compensation or better treatment, they could easily be replaced with some other workers. Ideally, under such conditions, workers would be compliant with management's every request.

This dream of workers as replaceable parts dates back at least as far as the Industrial Revolution. For example, Adam Smith's colleague, Adam Ferguson rhapsodized:

> Many mechanical arts, indeed, require no capacity; they succeed best under a total suppression of sentiment and reason; and ignorance is the mother of industry as well as of superstition. Reflection and fancy are subject to err; but a habit of moving the hand, or the foot, is independent of either. Manufacturers, accordingly, prosper, where the mind is least consulted, and where the workshop may, without any great effort of imagination, be considered as an engine, the parts of which are men. (Ferguson 1793, pp. 182-3)

Employers struggled mightily to eliminate the workers' monopoly of information. They had no intention of democratizing information. Instead, they merely wanted to gain an edge by reorganizing work in a way that they, not the workers, would possess the strategic information required to control the labor process. The most common method in this struggle was the adoption of machinery to replace workers with strategic skills with unskilled workers—often women and children (see Braverman 1974). Over time, management succeeded in gaining an increasing edge over labor insofar as the information about the production process was concerned.

Workers' recalcitrance put a further premium on information about workers' activities. As a result, a good deal of the requisite information was information about the workers themselves. As Alfred Marshall, probably the most influential economist of the early twentieth century, observed concerning the early firm, "The master's eye is everywhere;

there is no shirking by his foremen or workmen, no divided responsibility, no sending half-understood messages" (Marshall 1920, p. 284).

In Stephen Hymer's more forceful expression, the employer ideally "saw everything, knew everything, and decided everything" (Hymer 1972, p. 122). But then, the employer had relatively little to know compared to his modern day counterpart. Here is how Hymer compared the expanding span of capitalist control:

> [By Marshall's day, the] Marshallian capitalist ruled his factory from an office on the second floor. At the turn of the century, the president of a large national corporation was lodged in a higher building, perhaps on the seventh floor, with greater perspective and power. In today's giant corporation, managers rule from the top of skyscrapers; on a clear day, they can almost see the world. (Hymer 1972, p. 124)

In this new environment, economists suddenly began to treat control of information as an important component of the production process worthy of special compensation.

The Labor Process and the Control over Information

Workers clearly understood what was at stake in management's' efforts to gain control over strategic information. As Big Bill Haywood, the noted U.S. labor organizer, once proclaimed, "The manager's brains are under the workman's cap" (Haywood and Bohn, n.d., p. 25; cited in Montgomery 1979, p. 9). John Frey, an experienced iron molder and leading labor journalist, agreed. For him, "It is this unique possession of craft knowledge and craft skill on the part of a body of wage workers, that is, their possession of these things and the employers' ignorance of them, that has enabled the workers to organize and force better terms from the employers" (cited in Hoxie 1915, p. 131; and Livingston 1987, p. 78).

Naturally, workers resisted the introduction of new technologies, the purpose of which was to undermine the importance of workers' skills and information. Bloody battles ensued. In the end, management replaced skilled workers with new technologies, largely manned by unskilled workers, but including a few skilled employees, say to maintain a new machine. These new skilled workers developed their own strategic skills, requiring another round of efforts to deskill their jobs.

The strategic importance of deskilling was central to Frederick W. Taylor's efforts to create a "scientific management." Taylor clearly understood how labor used its strategic information to organize teams and monitor itself. For example, even when metal polishers were paid by the piece, they ensured that no one exceeded what the union considered to be a reasonable output. When some workers fell behind in their quota, their fellow workers would still earn the standard salary. Despite a complex pay schedule for different tasks, workers ended up with wages that differed by only a few pennies (Montgomery 1987, p. 152).

In short, management's victory was far from complete. In Taylor's words:

> In an industrial establishment that employs say from 500 to 1,000 workmen, there will be found in many cases at least twenty to thirty different trades. The workmen in each of these trades have had their knowledge handed down to them by word-of-mouth. . . . This mass of rule-of-thumb or traditional knowledge may be said to be the principal asset or possession of every tradesman.
>
> [The] foreman and superintendents [who comprise the management] know better than anyone else that their own knowledge and personal skill falls far short of the combined knowledge and dexterity of all the workmen under them.
>
> [I]n nineteen out of twenty industrial establishments, the workmen believe it to be directly against their interests to give their employers their best initiative. (Taylor 1911, pp. 31-2)

As a result, Taylor insisted that management had to discover new information that would give it the advantage over its labor force:

> . . . the deliberate gathering in on the part of those on the management's side of all the great mass of traditional knowledge, which in the past has been in the heads of the workmen, and in the physical skill and knack of the workmen, which he [sic] has acquired through years of experience. The duty of gathering in of [sic] all this great mass of traditional knowledge and recording it, tabulating it, and, in many cases, finally reducing it to laws, rules, and even to mathematical formulae, is voluntarily assumed by the scientific managers. (Taylor 1947, p. 40)

Even today, management has not completely mastered the workplace. According to Shoshana Zuboff, in older pulp and paper mills where she worked as a consultant, operators still use their bodies to regulate production. One man judged the condition of paper coming off a dry roller by the sensitivity of his hair to electricity in the atmosphere around the machine. Another could judge the moisture content of a roll of pulp by a quick slap of his hand. Another told her, "I used to listen to the sounds the boiler makes and know just how it was running. I could look at the fire in the furnace and tell by its color how it was burning. I knew what kinds of adjustment were needed by the shades of color I saw." In the words of still another worker, "I can chew pulp and tell you its physical properties. We know things from experience" (Zuboff 1988, pp. 58-63).

Science and the Labor Process

Let me now turn to an example of the sort of information that Taylor wanted to develop. Taylor's initial fame did not come from his efforts to manage workers directly, but rather from his discovery of information about the process of production that was superior to that of skilled workers. He owed his success, in part, to many years of experience on the shop floor. He also conducted more than 30,000 recorded experiments and countless unrecorded ones, which consumed almost 800,000 pounds of iron and steel (Shaiken 1985, pp. 23-4).

Along with White, a fellow engineer, he experimented on hardening metal for cutting tools. Machinists had long known from experience that metal should be heated until it turns "cherry red," then cooled quickly. They knew that further heating would destroy the temper of the metal. Such knowledge was typical of the enormous store of information concerning the production process that workers held.

Taylor and White heated the best available steel to temperatures far beyond the range of practical experience. Their experiments confirmed that heating beyond cherry red would have ill effects, but at 225 degrees, quite a bit higher than cherry red, they found that the metal hardens once more until a maximum hardness is reached just below melting point. Bethlehem Steel adopted this technique by 1900, six years before it was introduced to the world in Taylor and White's 1906 paper.

Taylor's discovery was noteworthy because its creation violated the precepts of trained workers' common sense knowledge. Its implication was that science had made traditional knowledge obsolete. Since the interests of the scientists supposedly would not differ from those of management, firms could gain power at the expense of their workers (see Montgomery 1987, p. 230).

Of course, Taylor was not the first to have seen that scientific results would displace rule-of-thumb techniques. Several decades before, Karl Marx had written about the same process whereby "the replacement of the rule of thumb by the conscious application of natural science" would take place much to labor's disadvantage (Marx 1977, p. 508). After all, both Marx and Taylor realized:

> The accumulation of the skill and knowledge (scientific power) of the workers themselves is the chief form of accumulation, and infinitely more important than the accumulation . . . of the existing objective conditions of this accumulated activity. These objective conditions are only nominally accumulated and must be constantly produced and consumed anew. (Marx 1963-1971, Pt 3, pp. 266-7)

In conclusion, when workers' self-organization was the norm, business interests acted energetically to limit that aspect of the labor process. For example, Taylor concluded:

> The art of cutting metals involves a true science of no small magnitude . . . so intricate that it is impossible for any machinist who is suited to running a lathe year in and year out either to understand it or to work according to its laws without the help of men who have made this their specialty. (Taylor 1911, p. 102)

Such strategic information about the labor process, which management accumulates, allows it to seize control of the workplace at the expense of labor. In the process, capital rather than labor becomes the dominant organizer of the production process. In addressing this transformation, Marx observed:

> The possibility of intelligent direction of production expands in one direction because it vanishes in many others. What the specialized workers lose is concentrated in the capital that confronts them. (Marx 1977, p. 482)

Notice how this reorganization of the workplace dovetails with the development of the notion of an information economy. The specialized workers are informational workers. Previously, when their informational work was the responsibility of "ordinary" workers, nobody took note of the difficulty or importance of such activity. Once this work became separated from the blue-collar workers and more under the control of management, it suddenly became essential to productivity.

In one sense, Taylor was absolutely correct. Hypothetically, if workers stubbornly held to their long-standing traditions without any willingness to change, productivity would stagnate. Workers had reason to be unenthusiastic about change since employers would tend to select changes that would disadvantage the workers.

However, Taylor's fears were unfounded. Productivity was already increasing rapidly well before Taylor appeared on the scene.

In another sense, Taylor was dead wrong. Ideally, ordinary work should not be far removed from science. All kinds of work should allow for learning and experimentation by workers.

Instead, business employs scientific principles in the workplace to reduce workers' autonomy, as we discussed earlier. As Harry Braverman noted:

> The more science is incorporated into the labor process, the less the worker understands of the process; the more sophisticated an intellectual product the machine becomes, the less control and comprehension of the machine the worker has. In other words, the more the worker needs to know in order to remain a human being at work, the less does he or she know. (Braverman 1974, p. 425)

The Incomplete Conquest of the Labor Process

Earlier, we encountered some pulp and paper workers, who heavily relied on taste, touch, and visual cues in their work. Zuboff's study of their skills came at a time when management was investing heavily in computers and other technology to upgrade their production processes. With the new technology, most workers in the industry no longer came in direct contact with their machinery. Instead, they watched computer screens to make sure that the plant was working as it was intended to do. Zuboff observed, "Accustomed to gauging their integrity in intimate measures of strain and sweat, these workers find that information technology has challenged their assumptions and thrown them into turmoil" (Zuboff 1988).

In part, their turmoil was understandable. She notes several cases in which the computer indicators were wrong. The workers knew it, but were told to trust the computers rather than their own experience (Zuboff 1988, pp. 85 and 89).

Some workers soon became comfortable with the transition to automation. Others could not make the adjustment at all. In either case, the collective experience of the past was lost.

A few managers knew the value of the experience that was going to waste. One told Zuboff:

> In the digester area, we used to have guys doing it who had an art. After we put the computers in, when they went down we could go to manual backup. People remembered how to run the digesters. Now if we try to go back, they can't remember what to do. They have lost the feel for it. (Zuboff 1988, p. 64)

In the case of Zuboff's pulp and paper mills, information-based technology was relatively successful in replacing workers' traditional skills, although this success came nearly a century after Taylor called for such a transformation. True, the system occasionally malfunctioned, giving incorrect information to the operators, causing materials to overflow. These problems were not terribly serious because the technology was relatively simple.

In other industries, the consequences of an imperfect informational system are more severe. Let us turn to a well-known example.

In 1977, Aerospace Corporation had reported to the Nuclear Regulatory Commission that the Three Mile Island control room was poorly engineered from a human-factor standpoint. The report was stamped "for future resolution" and forgotten. The authorities had other warnings about cooling valves, emergency pumps, and feed water systems.

Then, on 28 March 1979 at 4 A.M., a valve that regulated the feed water system inside the reactor stuck in the open position. Because it was so late, the operators were not functioning well. Water began to drain out at 220 gallons per minute.

The plant had a history of sticky valves, but a red light to indicate a stuck valve did not function. The plant had a total of more than 6,000 gauges, meters, lights, and alarms that ran for 900 square feet. More than 800 indicators set off warnings, but the operators had difficulty extracting information from the system.

The operators assumed that there was a system error rather than a problem in the reactor. Computer printouts took about four seconds to print each message. Since there were so many warning messages, the system fell behind (Haywood 1995, pp. 19-20).

Thus, at least in the case of Three Mile Island, management succeeded in the battle to minimize workers' information; but their victory was pyrrhic at best.

Economics and the Neglect of the Role of Information

Economic theory eventually took notice of these changes in the informational structure of production in ways that Taylor and his followers had never anticipated. Keep in mind that all considerations of the creation of intellectual property rights were entirely absent from Taylor's plan for scientific management.

I do not find any indication that Taylor intended to develop an alternative form of intellectual property for management. In fact, we might say that, by advocating a program to undermine the workers' stock of information, in effect, Taylor laid out a plan to destroy the intellectual property of workers. Indeed, Taylor could achieve his goal even if his managerial based knowledge were universally available. All that was required, so far as Taylor was concerned, was to break the workers' monopoly of knowledge.

So long as labor on the shop floor controlled the bulk of the information about the production process, economists never addressed the importance of information. Workers were not seen as repositories of information, but merely as shirkers who required managers to keep them diligent. Alfred Marshall was not alone in noting that managers had to be watchful, but watchfulness did not constitute information.

Nonetheless, economists did not see profits as a reward for watchfulness. For example, Adam Smith took pains to deny that profits were merely "a different name for the wages of a particular sort of labour, the labour of inspection and direction" (Smith 1776, I.vi.6, p. 66). Although some economists might recognize the importance of information for a merchant, information seemed to be irrelevant at the point of production. Some early economists did understand that risk and profits were related (see Cantillon 1755, Chapter 13), but none seemed to have associated the willingness to take risks with information.

As soon as management began to find ways to break the workers' monopoly of information and to establish themselves as a major source of production information, economists suddenly began to take note of the great importance of information. As Alfred Marshall observed:

> Capital consists in great part of knowledge and organisation: and of this part some part is private property and other part is not. . . . Knowledge is our most powerful engine of production; it allows us to subdue Nature and force her to satisfy our wants. . . . The distinction between public and private property in knowledge and organization is of great and growing importance: in some respects of more importance than that between public and private property in material things. (Marshall 1920, p. 138-9)

Information at the time had not commonly attained the status as private property. Marshall even hinted at the futility of private property in information, noting:

> . . . broad ideas and knowledge, which when once acquired pass speedily into common ownership; and become part of the collective wealth, in the first instance of the countries to which the industries specially affected belong, and ultimately to the whole world. (Marshall 1923, p. 175)

Despite the existence of a patent system, wealth and power rarely passed into the hands of inventors. In fact, many inventors hardly benefitted at all from their discoveries. Instead, the economy rewarded those who owned capital, either physical or financial capital. Even so, Marshall seemed to anticipate the changes that were afoot in the increasingly private control of information.

Unfortunately, neither Marshall nor any other economists at the time offered much guidance in this matter. Private knowledge was indeed becoming crucial. More important, knowledge was fast becoming part of capital, but nobody seemed to have a handle on the coming information revolution.

Economists' Belated Recognition of Information

While workers' information dominated the production process, we heard little or nothing about the importance of information from economists. Only after management began to take more control of production did we hear the first hints about the importance of information. The iconoclastic Thorstein Veblen may have been the first major economist to suggest that information was the key to the effective use of capital. According to Veblen:

> These productive goods are facts of human knowledge, skill, and predilection; that is to say, they are, substantially, prevalent of thought and it is as such that they enter into the process of industrial development. The physical properties of the materials accessible to man are constant: it is the human agent that changes—his insight and his appreciation of what these things can be used for is what develops.
>
> It is in the human material that the continuity of development is to be looked for; and it is here, therefore, that the motor forces of the process of economic development must be studied if they are to be studied in action at all. (Veblen 1898, pp. 230-1)

Two decades later, Alfred Marshall continued on the same theme in his statement that we cited earlier:

> Capital consists in great part of knowledge and organisation: and of this part some part is private property and other part is not. Knowledge is our most powerful engine of production; it allows us to subdue Nature and force her to satisfy our wants. (Marshall 1920, p. 138)

Neither Veblen nor Marshall clearly addressed the question as to who owned the information, but so long as the information remained in the hands of the workers, we heard virtually nothing about information.

Once management had begun to succeed in displacing labor as the key repository of information, economic theory began to teach that management deserved to be rewarded for its possession of information. Under the presumption that management alone was suited to monitor or organize production teams, economists suddenly began to single out the ability to monitor or organize teams of workers as worthy of special compensation.

A few decades thereafter, economists began to emphasize the importance of education rather than the specific sort of knowledge that workers had about production. Economists referred to what workers did know about the production process as on-the-job training—something that the firm "gave" to the workers.

Economists, ever anxious to make everything fit into the framework of their theory, invented the concept of human capital—meaning the productive potential of the skills accumulated during the educational process. Theodore Schultz, who won a Nobel prize for his efforts along these lines, observed:

> Laborers have become capitalists not from a diffusion of the ownership of corporate stocks, as folklore would have it, but from the acquisition of knowledge and skill that have economic value. The knowledge and skill are in great part the product of investment and, combined with other human investment, predominately account for the productive superiority of advanced countries. (Schultz 1961, p. 3)

Learning by Doing

People do not just learn from books and lectures. They also learn by their own experience. We can see the importance of this sort information by watching people perfect their abilities to operate machinery and other equipment. Economists sometimes refer to this phenomenon as the Horndal effect, based on observations of the Swedish steel works at Horndal in the 15 years following its construction in 1935-1936. The company made no further investment in the facility save bare maintenance. Even so, according to one observer:

> During a period of 15 years beginning in the mid-1930s, one of the steel works (Horndal) of the Fagersta concern was neglected. No new investments were made except for a minimum of repairs and broken equipment replacement (without modernization). In spite of this, there was an annual increase in man-hour production of 2 percent during this period. This compares to a production growth per man-hour of 4 percent for the whole concern. In other plants of the company, significant new

investments were made during this time. (Lundberg 1961, pp. 130-1; cited in Lazonick and Brush 1985, pp. 53-4)

This common phenomenon, which Arrow explained as "learning by doing," is not unique to the Horndal plant (Arrow 1962a). Paul David found also found evidence of learning by doing in the nineteenth century textile industry at Lawrence Mill Number 2. He reported, "Detailed inventories of machines at times of purchase and in place in 1867, show that this mill worked with just about the same stock of machines between 1835 (when it was new) and 1856. Other company records show no changes in power plant, or the mill itself, between these two dates" (McGouldrick 1968; cited in David 1975, p. 176).

Engineers have observed similar trends in the airframe industry (Alchian 1963; and Wright 1936). Wright proposed an 80 percent rule for the industry: a doubling of production decreases average costs to 80 percent of their initial level (Wright 1936, pp. 124-5).

The experiences at Horndal and Lawrence Mill #2 are not surprising. Students of industrial practices have long known that machinery frequently runs better the second year than when it is first installed (Naysmith 1852; cited in Marx 1862, pp. 411-2; Pakes and Griliches 1984; and Sylos-Labini 1983-1984, p. 173). Over a longer period, old equipment might undergo some modernization through partial replacement, but the association of productivity increases with a static capital stock is still significant.

The ability for economies to rebound after disasters perhaps represents the strongest evidence for the importance of the sort of information that people develop from learning by doing. For example, in the middle of the nineteenth century, John Stuart Mill remarked on

> [the] excited wonder [surrounding] the great rapidity with which countries recover from a state of devastation; the disappearance, in a short time, of all traces of the mischiefs done by earthquakes, floods, hurricanes, and the ravages of war. An enemy lays waste a country by fire and sword, and destroys or carries away nearly all the moveable wealth existing in it: all the inhabitants are ruined, and yet in a few years after, everything is much as it was before. (Mill 1848, p. 74)

In a particularly dramatic example, Jack Hirshleifer reported that ten days of bombing raids during July and August 1943 destroyed half the buildings in Hamburg. Yet, within five months the city had regained up to 80 percent of its productive capacity (Hirshleifer 1987, pp. 12-3).

In the last days of February 1944, the Allies targeted the German aircraft plants. They destroyed the buildings, but the machine tools remained relatively intact. New assembly lines were organized in nearby buildings. In March, 48 percent more planes were produced than in February (Galbraith 1994, p. 130; also 1981, p. 205). Bombs just seemed to make the people more resolute (Scitovsky 1991, p. 258).

On 6 August 1945, the United States Air Force dropped an atomic bomb on Hiroshima. The next day, electric power service was restored to surviving areas. One week later, telephone service restarted (Hirshleifer 1987, p. 13-4).

No doubt the Germans and the Japanese worked overtime to rebuild their economic capacity, but even trebling the average workday would not have sufficed to accomplish what they did. Their success in reconstructing their economies also required a combination of information, together with enormous creativity and ingenuity.

Why can a war-torn Japan or Germany rebuild in a few years, while other societies make little or no economic progress, even in the absence of war? Some of these lagging economies suffer under enormous exploitation and corruption, but the core answer lies elsewhere. Once you have the requisite knowledge to build up a modern economy, rebuilding is not terribly difficult.

We should not take this idea so far that we get tangled up with George Gilder's previously cited idea that "The powers of mind are everywhere ascendant over the brute force of things" (Gilder 1989, p. 18). Information alone is not magical. The ravages of war kept the Japanese and German economies in poverty for years after the end of the war. Information, however, did allow them to rebound far faster than anyone could have imagined.

The Labor Process and the Learning Process

Here we come to one of the fundamental conflicts between the market and the information economy. Despite the importance of information in the production process, managers have strategic reasons to limit workers' access to information. While society as a whole could benefit from workers' knowledge, modern managers and owners of industry become more valuable to the extent that they have exclusive control of indispensable information about their business.

Just as the Egyptian priests gained influence and power from their exclusive knowledge about the timing of the flooding of the Nile, managers and owners of business benefit from the exclusivity of their information. From their perspective, if workers had their own exclusive and indispensable information, they could demand higher compensation, probably at the expense of management. In this sense, control over information becomes a determinant of class as much as ownership of capital.

Firms do not just use information to facilitate production. They also use their information to improve their control over labor in the workplace. While close supervision and control can instill enough fear in many workers to make them work hard, these same conditions can also stifle creativity.

In 1911, when the United States House of Representatives was hearing testimony about Frederick Taylor's system of management, Samuel Gompers, then head of the American Federation of Labor, warned the congressman that scientific management might promise a greater output of "goods and things, but insofar as the men are concerned, it means destruction" (Gompers 1911, p. 27; see also Kanigel 1997, p. 449). Gompers continued:

> Mr. Vreeland, you spoke about planning the work of a factory so as to avoid the taking of unnecessary steps. Now, that is very true so far as steps are concerned, but it is also true that the time that a man ordinarily devotes to extra steps or an extra motion is frequently that moment when the divine spark of a new thought comes to him. . . . That brief leisure time, the minute, the half-minute, or the ten seconds of mental and physical relaxation is necessary in order to get the best results. (Gompers 1911, p. 32)

No doubt, hard work is important in production, but creativity is required if we are to expand our economic potential significantly. Discipline can make a worker put in the equivalent of an extra few hours on any one day, but a single great idea can save millions of hours of work in the future.

Of course, nobody would recommend a workforce in which all were free to spend all of their time daydreaming in search of some creative inspiration. Even so, some time for focused contemplation can pay huge dividends. In this sense, the close supervision and control so beloved by management is ultimately self-defeating (see Gordon 1996).

Work proceeds best when it is both interesting and challenging; where workers have a sense of their own dignity. These conditions call for a degree of autonomy for workers. Even before workers enter the workplace, they should have the benefit of stimulating education to nurture their creative potential. Instead, we have deadening schools to prepare workers for deadening work.

The Example of the Machine Tool Industry

The struggle in the machine tool industry between record-playback (R/P) and numerical control (N/C) illustrates clearly the struggle over who will control information in the workplace (Noble 1984). R/P technology is similar to a macro in word processing, in which a series of the computer repeats upon command a series of keystrokes that the user has already entered. In R/P, the worker's manipulations are recorded. The machine can play these back upon command.

In N/C technology, a programmer working in a back office defines what the machine is supposed to do. The worker's role is reduced to watching over the machine just to make sure that nothing goes wrong.

At the end of World War II, R/P technology was the more promising of the two alternatives. Both business and the United States Air Force pushed the N/C technology for one reason: It reduced the importance of the machinist. In David Noble's words, "Whereas record-playback was a reproducer, and, thus a multiplier of skill, extending the reach of the machinist, N/C was an abstract synthesizer of skill, circumventing and eliminating altogether the need for the machinist" (Noble 1984, p. 84).

Noble describes the work of Ralph Kuhn, tool and die supervisor and member of the value engineering department in the Dearborn tool and die shop of Ford's River Rouge complex. His simple "trace and record" method was much more efficient than the Ford N/C engineers but Ford poured money into the N/C alternative instead of Kuhn's system (Noble 1984, pp. 183-5). Noble concluded, "Management did not want to yield such a measure of control to workers and their organization."

Noble quotes a number of sources to indicate that this attitude was quite common in industrial circles. For example, Alan A. Smith of Arthur D. Little enthused that N/C signals "our emancipation from human workers" (Noble 1984, p. 235). In an article entitled "What is Numerical Control?" in the 25 October 1984 issue of the trade magazine *American Machinist,* we find, "Numerical control is not a strictly metalworking technique, it is a philosophy of control" (Noble 1984, pp. 237-8). Similarly, in a 30 August 1976 article in *Iron Age* entitled "Machine Tools that Are Building America," the author concluded, "The fundamental advantages of numerical control [is that it] brings production control to the Engineering Department" (Noble 1984, p. 238).

Although N/C has made great progress in part by taking advantage of advances in computer technology, we cannot be sure that the machine tool industry would not have been superior today, if it had first perfected the R/P system before making the switch to N/C technology. In any case, the story of the development of the machine tool nicely illustrates how the struggle for informational control affects the evolution of technology.

Science and Property Rights in Information

If we do not provide workers with the opportunity to discover new and better ways of producing, then we must pin all of our hopes on science. How, then, can we best promote scientific progress?

Four centuries before the Age of Taylorism, some states had already begun to encourage scientific discovery through patents. Undoubtedly, patent rights can be a significant incentive for corporations, but, of course, corporations do not engage in science—people do, even if those people happen to be working for a corporation. Yes, corporations may pay their salaries and even structure their priorities, but scientists and engineers do the actual work.

Recently, even with the lure of patents and the promise of a coming information age, many of the great corporations in the United States have begun to skimp on research. This strategy has contributed to widespread unemployment and underemployment among scientists.

Rather than investing in science, the great corporations seem to prefer to use their funds for financial manipulation. In a study of 250 firms in the United States that had increased their debt significantly, total industrial research and development spending fell 2.5 percent, or about one billion 1982 dollars, despite all the protection of intellectual property rights (Stiglitz 1994).

We will do better to reframe the question about patents: How do we organize society so that we develop an ability to use our technological and scientific resources most effectively? We should note with respect to this question that science and business practices are often incompatible.

Suppose we had set out on a safari to observe our great scientific researchers at their places of work before the corporatization of science began. Let us imagine that we had been stalking them in the halls of a great university to study them in the process of creating science.

We would have discovered some of our quarry in their offices, reading preprints of the latest scientific discovery or scanning the Net for new breakthroughs. We could have found others hard at work in their laboratories. Such activities conform to the common perception about how scientists create science.

Other researchers might have eluded our hunt by blending into the landscape. A seasoned eye might have located them casually chatting away, indistinguishable from any other supposedly idle workers apparently loafing on the job. Imagine that we stopped to listen more closely. Some of their exchanges might be integrally related to their work (Center for Workplace Development 1998). Derry Roopenian, a biologist at the Jackson Laboratory in Bar Harbor, Maine reminisced about those times:

> At one time, if you found something exciting, you would run down the corridor and talk about it. . . . Now if you discover something but a commercial backer is interested in it, you can't say a word about it. (Gibbs 1996)

Other conversations would seem to have nothing whatsoever to do with their work. For example, Francis Crick and Sydney Brenner, who won the Nobel Prize in medicine in 1965, shared an office for twenty years. They had the rule of uttering "anything that came into your head." According to Brenner, much of their conversation was "just complete nonsense [but] . . . every now and then a half-formed idea could be taken up by the other and really refined" (Stephan and Levin 1992, p. 15; citing Wolpert and Richards 1988, p. 106).

Unfortunately, we, just like Crick and Brenner, would probably be unable to distinguish between the idle and the productive exchanges. In many cases, seemingly frivolous chatter could turn out to be a central part of the scientific discovery. In such conversations, workers might learn how the others think. A random remark about something as trivial as a sporting event can spark a stunning scientific breakthrough.

Those who manage the university cannot control such exchanges. Even so, qualities, such as friendship, trust, and conviviality, can facilitate scientific and technological progress. Absence of these same qualities can promote secrecy and even attempts to throw fellow workers off the track.

Of course, in science as elsewhere, some, including some of the greatest figures, are selfish and even antisocial. These traits may even help those individuals to rise above the rest of their fellow workers, but they will not be likely to promote the overall level of progress. Scientific progress will proceed the fastest where scientists cooperate and share information while vying for recognition among their peers.

While scientific progress is no doubt important, those who have studied the evolution of technology insist that incremental improvements in technology are even more crucial to technical progress than the more dramatic scientific discoveries. Of course, both kinds of progress are important and both require openness that is incompatible with the narrow pursuit and acquisition of intellectual property.

Orwellian Freedom in the Information Age Workplace

Karl Marx once noted with bitter irony that the typical employer-employee relationships necessarily required freedom, so much so that the "worker must be free in the double sense" (Marx 1977, p. 272). By "double sense," Marx meant that while workers had to be free to sell their labor on the market, they also had to be free of ownership of capital or any alternatives to wage labor. Otherwise, they would avoid wage relationships altogether because freedom is nonexistent on the ideal shop floor.

This sphere of double freedom in the workplace has continued to expand. Despite considerable unemployment, more and more people feel compelled to work more and more hours in the contemporary United States (Schor 1991). In fact, recurrent unemployment contributes to the need for periods of extensive overwork (Bluestone and Rose 1997). Within this realm of freedom, employers are enjoying a rapidly expanding ability to keep watch over their employees. Today, an employer can monitor every keystroke of his employees.

In a sense, such powers are not altogether new. Charles Babbage, who had designed a prototype of the computer in the early nineteenth century, observed at the time:

> One great advantage which we may derive from machinery is from the check which it affords against the inattention, the idleness or the dishonesty of human agents. . . . Perhaps the most useful contrivance of this kind is one for ascertaining the vigilance of a watchman. It is a piece of mechanism connected with a clock placed in an apartment to which the watchman has no access; but he is ordered to pull a string situated in a certain part of his round once in every hour. The instrument, aptly called a tell-tale, informs the owner whether the man has missed any, and what hours, during the night. (Babbage 1835, pp. 54-5)

Of course, as Stephen Hymer noted, the capacity for watchfulness has progressed enormously since the time of Babbage or even since the days of Marshall. Contemporary employers can peruse their employees' e-mail and listen to their voice mail. They can test the hair or urine of their workforce to see if their employees have ingested any illegal substances. They are even beginning to test the genetic makeup of their potential employees. And the beat goes on.

In an Orwellian sense, the information age has increased the sphere of freedom. Despite the great promise of the information age, many workers are suddenly discovering new dimensions of freedom. They are finding themselves free of medical care. Others are suddenly finding themselves free of their pensions and other encumbrances of modern life.

Millions of workers are even finding themselves free of a job, as unemployment becomes more common. For example, in the face of an International Labor Organization report that estimated 30 percent of the world's labor force is unemployed or underemployed, the *Wall Street Journal* noted that "many management theorists" regard the analysis as outdated because "the whole concept of a job—steady work at steady pay from the same employer—must be discarded" (Zachary 1995; see also Bridges 1994a and 1994b).

For example, just after AT&T announced the layoff of 40,000 workers, James Meadows, a vice president for human resources, responsible for the policy, explained:

> In AT&T, we have to promote the whole concept of the workforce being contingent, though most of our contingent workers are inside our walls. Jobs [are being replaced by] projects [and] fields of work [are giving rise to a society that is increasingly] jobless but not workless.
>
> People need to look at themselves as self-employed, as vendors who come to this company to sell their skills. (Andrews 1996)

Today corporations commonly fire hordes of skilled white-collar workers, then turn around and offer to rehire them as independent contractors at a slightly higher wage, but without any benefits or job security.

This environment makes many workers so fearful that they cede to their employers an increasing amount of their time. Many new factories work longer hours, requiring the abandonment of the eight-hour day (Kilborn 1996). Laptops, cellular phones, and modems allow workers to be on the job virtually twenty four hours a day. As workers move to more irregular hours, coordination of family life becomes more difficult, if not impossible.

Modern information technologies are not merely instruments that allow employers to take advantage of their workforce. In industry after industry, these same technologies also make harsh working conditions imperative. In the electronic age, investors and speculators can move money across the globe in an instant in search of the highest possible profit. If any firm fails to live up to heightened profit expectations, investors will desert it in droves and takeover artists will attempt to capture the firm and dispose of the current managers. In this environment, management must be ever vigilant to find new ways to increase profits.

The madcap pursuit of profits might mean moving jobs abroad where workers earn a dollar or two per day, or it might mean lethal exposure of workers to toxic chemicals. In any case, profits remain uppermost.

Yes, the information age has the potential to make us free. New technologies could lighten the workload and make leisure plentiful. Instead, the computer has both unleashed the Orwellian potential of the workplace and made working conditions deteriorate.

Knowledge, Information, and Classes

Although early economists did not treat information as an important part of the production process, education was a central factor in the formation of classes. Economists, from Adam Smith through Marshall, saw the typical worker as an unrefined brute. In the earlier, less subtle variants of this proposition, a class structure sorted the brutes from the sophisticates. For example, Smith's colleague, Adam Ferguson, whom we met earlier, proposed:

> In every commercial state, notwithstanding any pretension to equal rights, the exaltation of a few must depress the many. In this arrangement, we think that the extreme meanness of some classes must arise chiefly from the defect of knowledge, and of liberal education; and we refer to such classes, as to an image of what our species must have been in its rude and uncultivated state. (Ferguson 1793, p. 186)

Education, according to Smith and many of his followers, would somehow refine the working classes. The economists were vague about the ultimate consequences of the edification of the working class. My own suspicion is that they did not expect that the prosperous strata of society would welcome the rebellious working classes into their ranks unconditionally; instead, they cherished the hope that the working classes would abandon their antagonism toward the market and embrace commercial society.

Of course, these economists were not so foolish as to think that they could do without a working class. A more realistic reading of their perspective would propose that education would make the class system more porous, allowing some of the more ambitious workers to move into a more affluent state. In this manner, education would also make the system of classes more durable by providing a safety valve for the more ambitious, thereby diminishing the workers' recalcitrance.

During the period in which Ferguson and Smith were writing, the typical skilled industrial worker did not live a very different life from his employer. Their suggestion that education could somehow remove the bit from the class system did not sound outlandish at the time, but the times were already changing.

The share of skilled workers in the total industrial population was falling. In the dominant industry of the age—textiles—management already had accumulated sufficient information to capture a position of dominance. Employers structured their factories so that they could hire children to do the bulk of the work.

The income from ownership had begun to far outstrip the income from industrial labor, even labor based on skill. Over time, this gulf between income streams has continued to widen even though workers' educational levels continued to improve.

While the early industrialists made their fortunes by dint of their ruthless ambition, much wealth passed into the hands of their descendants, who enjoyed the pleasures of the idle rich. Why should workers not feel resentment over their circumstances? Not surprisingly, economics had a ready answer: the economy works through the cooperative efforts of workers, who supply the labor, and employers, who supply the capital. Needless to say, few workers found this theory convincing.

A Failed Resolution of Conflict within the Firm

The traditional defense of the relationship between workers and employers makes even less sense in the context of the information age, where material capital is less consequential and employers supposedly hire workers for their information. What then does the employer bring to the table?

Richard Nelson and Sidney Winter set out to explain away the conflictive nature of the employment relationship by reformulating the image of the firm in their influential book, *An Evolutionary Theory of Economic Change* (1982). They minimize worker's information. From their perspective, the role of firms is merely to accumulate information and design rules that routinize many of the activities within the firm in a neutral way that favors neither workers nor management.

Nelson and Winter do not acknowledge that this concentration of information is an artificial construction, in which the corporation systematically creates barriers to prevent workers from having access to information. On the contrary, they contend that firms stand above any conflict. In their opinion, firms do not act in the interest of any particular group. Within the context of the routines that the firms develop, they propose that the firm has the ability to organize a voluntary cessation of outright conflict among

its employees. Here is their description of the manner in which firms eliminate intrafirm conflict:

> In routine operation, the combined effect of the rule-enforcement
> mechanism and other motivators is such as to leave members content
> to play their roles in the organization routine. . . . [T]hey are willing to
> continue to perform up to their usual standard, to the accompaniment
> of the usual amount of griping and squabbling. Conflict, both manifest
> and latent, persists, but manifest conflict follows largely predictable
> paths and stays within predictable bounds that are consistent with the
> ongoing routine. In short, routine operation involves a comprehensive
> truce in intraorganizational conflict. There is a truce between the su-
> pervisor and those supervised at every level in the organizational hier-
> archy: the usual amount of work gets done, reprimands and
> compliments are delivered with the usual frequency, and no demands
> are presented for major modification in the terms of the relationship.
> (Nelson and Winter 1982, p. 189)

In effect, Nelson and Winter invert the roles of the human workers and inhuman firms. From their perspective, individuals do not hold the most
important information within the firm. Instead, they describe the firm as
a suprahuman institution brain, something akin to H. G. Wells's World
Brain, which we shall discuss below.

Let us place Nelson and Winter in the context of our earlier discussion
about the ambiguity of the ownership of information with the firm. A
quarter century before their book appeared, Graaf broached this subject
in a very abstract book, entitled, *Theoretical Welfare Economics* (1957).
His concern was about the technical refinement of a theoretical model of
production. Almost in passing, he innocuously remarked, "In itself a firm
possesses no knowledge. That which is available to it belongs to the men
associated with it" (Graaf 1957, p. 16).

Graaf's assertion inadvertently stirred up an ideological hornet's nest, at
least as far as Sidney Winter was concerned, even though Winter took several decades before he responded to Graaf's words. Winter first rebuked
Graaf for his seemingly unobjectionable assertion, proclaiming, ". . . it is
the firms, not the people who work for the firms, that know how to make
gasoline, automobiles, and computers" (Winter 1982, p. 76), but a couple
of pages later he tempered his position, acknowledging, "I conclude that
there is much merit both in the view that individuals are repositories of productive knowledge and in the view that business firms and other organizations are such repositories" (Winter 1982, p. 78). A few years later, Winter
repeated his earlier critique of Graaf, but this time without any qualification (Winter 1991, p. 185).

Why does Winter keep repeating his critique of Graaf? Let us turn again to the sage Kenneth Arrow, who, without reference to Winter observed:

> What is the role of the firm in standard economic theory? It is a locus of knowledge, as embodied in a production possibility set. But where is this knowledge located and in what sense is it characteristic of the firm? Some of the knowledge that is most important is largely embodied in individuals. (Arrow 1996, p. 126)

Here we come to the rub. Arrow continues:

> The embodiment of knowledge in workers contradicts the standard theoretical meaning of a firm. In the neoclassical model, workers are not part of the firm. They are inputs purchased on the market, like raw materials or capital goods. Yet they carry the firm's information base, even though not permanently attached to the firm. Defining the firm as a locus of productive knowledge leads to a dilemma; what knowledge is peculiar to a firm. (Arrow 1996, p. 126)

Like Arrow, Winter realized that Graaf's perspective threatened the structure of economic theory. More important, Graaf's approach called into question the entire distribution of income.

Nelson and Winter do not take kindly to such questions. They stand ready to defend traditional economic theory, as well as the distribution of income. They take for granted the present arrangement whereby owners of information as capital, rather than labor, reap the great rewards that flow from that information. They justify this situation by proposing that firms, not individuals, are the repositories of knowledge. Firms' great rewards are merely the returns to the store of information that they have accumulated.

Certainly we have come a long way from the time when economists failed to recognize the role of information in the productive process. The question remains as to whether or not that evolution in the theory of information constituted progress.

4

The Contradiction of Exploited Informational Labor

Software Morass

Software is not just for computers. It is everywhere. A television set may contain up to 500 kilobytes of software; an electric shaver, two (Gibbs 1994, p. 88).

The automobile illustrates the expanding role of software. The volume of code is exploding as processors proliferate behind the dashboard and under the hood. The power trains in new General Motors cars run 30,000 lines of computer code (Gibbs 1994, p. 88). An engine controller can have 100,000 lines of code (Costlow 1996, p. 156). In comparison, an on-line version of Shakespeare's collected works contains just over 175,000 lines.

The typical auto has 10 to 15 processors; high-end cars can have as many as 80. William Powers, vice president of research at Ford, noted: "Software is where the problem is today. . . . Today, if you change a line of code, you're looking at the potential for some major problems. Hardware is very predictable, very repeatable. Software is in much more of a transient state" (Costlow 1996, p. 156).

Programmers often must work closely with the intended user so that they can take into account a wide array of factors that would probably not occur to a technically inclined programmer working in isolation. For example, Mitch Kapor, founder of Lotus, reported that management expected it would take nine months to adapt its 1-2-3 spreadsheet into a Japanese version. It took more than two years and cost $5 million more than expected because of cultural incompatibility. The Japanese record dates in terms of years of the emperor. They would be offended by any provision to allow a new dating to begin with a new emperor. To do so would suggest that the emperor might be mortal. The U.S. version of the program beeps to indicate mistakes. The Japanese would lose face if others could hear a user's computer beep (Kapor 1989, p. 44).

A decade ago, Edward Yourdon, who later wrote *The Decline and Fall of the American Programmer* (1992), estimated that large software projects are typically 100 percent over budget and one year behind schedule (Carroll 1987). Since then, matters have grown even worse.

> For every six new large-scale software systems, two others are canceled. The average software development project overshoots its schedule by half; larger projects do worse. Three quarters of all large systems are "operating failures" that either do not function as intended or are not used at all. (Gibbs 1994, p. 86)

> For example, in 1987, California's Department of Motor vehicles decided to merge its state driver's license and vehicle registration systems. It had hoped to develop convenient one-stop renewal kiosks. Instead, it saw the projected costs explode 6.5 times its expected price and the delivery date to recede to 1988. In December, the agency pulled the plug and walked away from the 17 year, $44.3 million investment. (Gibbs 1994, p. 89)

The Federal Aviation Administration's project to replace the nation's obsolete air-traffic control system is a well-known software quagmire. The agency expected to pay about $100 per line of code, five times the industry average. It ended up paying $700 to $900 per line. Each line had to be rewritten twice (Gibbs 1994, p. 89).

In June 1994, the agency decided to cancel two of four major parts and to scale back a third. The $144 million spent on these failed programs paled next to the $1.4 billion invested on the fourth and central piece: A new work station software for air-traffic controllers. It is now more than five years late and more than $1 billion over budget (Gibbs 1994, p. 89).

The British air traffic control project is experiencing similar problems. The project consists of about a million lines of code, containing about 15,000 bugs (Doyle 1997).

Once a large program is completed, the work is far from done. Errors in code are inevitable. Locating these errors often represents an enormous challenge. A billing system for a utility requires about one million lines of code. Just imagine the complexity of the search for an error hidden within a million lines of computer code. As a result, corporate programmers now spend 80 percent of their time just repairing software and updating it to keep it running (Carroll 1987).

Some of the problems that crop up might be fairly trivial. Others are not. A single misplaced keystroke may suffice to create a disaster.

The Vulnerability of Complex Systems

We have already seen the paradoxical situation in which our supposed information economy denies people access to information. We have discussed how corporations deny workers access to information to maintain power over their employees. Since public education has long been the primary information delivery mechanism in our society, we can say that the decline in the educational system represents an additional barrier to informational access.

This paradox of accessibility of information takes on frightening dimensions when we consider that one of the most striking aspects of the information economy is the degree to which we find ourselves dependent upon complex systems. Whether we are passengers in a jumbo jet or patients relying on a sophisticated medical device, our very survival frequently requires that our modern technology work flawlessly.

Often, these complex systems share two distressing qualities: First, they are brittle; second, the failure of even a seemingly insignificant part can cause a horrible disaster (Perrow 1984). A single weld in a giant airplane or a single misplaced character in a million-line program can cause a catastrophe. Happily, in most cases tragedy does not occur, but increasingly often it does.

Ominously, as the systems on which we depend become ever more complex, the failures will become still more common, unless we learn to improve the way that we organize the development of complex systems. To prevent disasters, we require an adequate assessment of risks and a competent labor force.

Let us turn to the former concern. Perhaps the most spectacular disaster was the explosion of the Challenger spacecraft. Richard Feynman, the famous physicist who is credited with discovering that a defective O-ring was responsible for the explosion, also noted that the people in charge of the space program were (willfully?) ignorant of the risks associated with their project.

According to Feynman, Louis J. Ullian, the range safety officer at Kennedy Space Center, where the Challenger launch occurred, said that 5 of 127 previous rockets had failed, representing about four percent of the total flights. Ullian assumed that unmanned flights would be safer, so he figured a one-percent failure rate. The National Aeronautics and Space Administration told him that the probability of failure was 1 in 100,000. Ullian could never figure how the agency arrived at its estimate (Feynman 1988, p. 179).

The Challenger case was unusual in one respect. A hardware function caused its demise. Peter Neumann's unsettling book, *Computer Related Risks,* lists 15 serious problems that occurred in the United States manned space program. Of these, nine seemed to involve a software problem (Neumann 1995, p. 32).

Here we have an extraordinarily toxic mixture. Such projects are inherently risky. Any one of thousands of parts is capable of causing a tragedy. Over and above the danger of a mechanical failure, such flights are dependent on extraordinarily complex computer software.

The best-known spacecraft catastrophe due to a software error occurred with the Mariner I spacecraft, the first U.S. space vehicle designed to visit another planet (Venus). On the morning of 22 July 1962, the space vehicle rocketed from the launch pad and four minutes into its flight began moving on an erratic path. NASA had to destroy it in the air before it could do any serious damage. A single incorrect character in the equations of motion encoded in a huge FORTRAN guidance program was responsible for the failure (Campbell-Kelly and Aspray 1996, p. 200).

The Challenger and the Mariner incidents teach us the importance of care and competence in complex systems. They also suggest a less obvious lesson with more far-reaching consequences: The dictates of the market and the characteristics of modern technology may be incompatible.

A probably apocryphal story illustrates this incompatibility. A woman who cleaned hospital rooms was unable to find an unused electrical outlet to run her buffer. When she ran into this problem, she would simply unplug a cord from one of the outlets, complete her job, and then methodically reattach the cord, but not before patients on life support had expired.

Tracing even this simple problem would not be a trivial matter. Presumably, the affected patients would have only two things in common: reliance on electricity for life support and a shortage of electrical outlets in their room. The first is obvious; the second is not. Who would think to check for the absence of a spare electrical outlet when assessing the cause of death?

In the case of the person who cleaned the room, a hospital could publish a set of guidelines. If the hospital management were somehow to think through all the contingencies, it could develop a standard procedure that would prevent the cleaner from making a fatal decision. As we have seen, Nelson and Winter (1982) suggest that the creation of such routines is central to the functioning of a firm.

No hospital administration would be able to anticipate all contingencies. I suspect that the spare outlet problem would be among the possibilities that management would be likely to overlook. Given that one small mistake on the part of one of a large number of workers can result in a disaster in many complex systems, employers in such cases might be expected to pay premium wages in order to attract the best workers and to keep them motivated (Kremer 1993).

With modern technological systems, a product may have no value (or may even impose a large cost) unless a multitude of tasks are all completed competently. In addition, as we have noted, pinpointing the mistake that has caused failure is a difficult matter. Anticipating the problem is several orders of magnitude more difficult. As the single character in the faulty Mariner program suggested, nowhere are the dangers of complex systems more obvious than in the production of huge software projects.

Why Software Fails

The success of large software projects, rather than their failure, should be more a subject of surprise. As Frederick Brooks, who was project manager for its development and later as manager of the massive Operating System/360 software project for IBM, wrote, "The large programming effort . . . consists of many tasks, some chained end-to-end. The probability that each will go well becomes vanishingly small" (Brooks 1975, p. 16).

In a sense, we can compare the end product of a successful software project to a book, but a very special kind of book. A single ungrammatical sentence or a misplaced comma can make this kind of book fail, or even kill hundreds of readers. Even though modern authors can avail themselves of spell checkers, I rarely find a book that seems to be entirely free of all typographical or grammatical errors. Most likely, when I do, the errors are there, but I am just overlooking them.

In a book, the interpretation of a simple declarative sentence is relatively straightforward. In the program, many of the lines of code are complex mathematical statements. Even for a skilled programmer, interpreting the "meaning" of this code may take considerable skill.

The program differs from a book in another respect. Each of the lines of code in the program must be consistent with all the other statements. A statement in one place may have serious but unexpected ramifications in other parts. Consistency is all the more difficult because numerous authors collaborate on these projects. To make matters worse, weeks or months may pass before the error becomes apparent. Then comes the difficult part—searching for the problem.

If two authors work together on a project, they might be able to communicate with each other. If their number expands the number of lines of communication multiplies by a factor of n(n-l)/2. To make matters worse, many of these authors work in far-flung regions of the plant, connected only by satellite communication. With the bureaucratization and geographical dispersion of programming, programmers lose the sort of informal face-to-face communication that often inspires great bursts of creativity.

Remember that nobody writes these large-scale computer programs for their own sake. They may be intended to organize an air traffic system or to monitor a medical device. Given the stakes involved in software production, you would think that those responsible for managing the programmers would want to employ the most skilled programmers available and to ensure that they enjoy their work. Surprisingly, many of those in charge of software production dismiss that approach. Instead, they want to drive workers in a manner comparable to what you can find in a sweatshop.

From time to time, I hear of frustrated programmers venting their frustration by slipping a harmless mark of their own individuality into a computer program. For example, they might insert a risqué image in a fast-moving scene in a computer game.

We can only wonder how this frustration might reflect itself in more vital programming projects. Most of us would not appreciate having our lives in the hands of a distraught surgeon or airline pilot. We would want these professionals to work in environments that they would enjoy. Today, the work of these professionals depends more and more on the prior work of programmers, whose efforts are just as crucial to our safety.

The Japanese Software Factory

How, then, can an organization be sure that its programmers will produce high-quality work, especially when the risks of failure can be so high? Some experts recommend what we might call the Japanese model.

Japanese programmers have a reputation for producing excellent software. In a few cases, Japanese software has been delivered with 100 times fewer errors than typical American software (Yourdon 1992, p. 7).

Michael Cusumano's study of Japanese programming presents perhaps the most influential case in favor of the Japanese model. Based on a sample of 20 U.S. and 11 Japanese firms, he finds that Japanese programmers produced 60 to 70 percent more lines of code. Defects per line of delivered code in the Japanese sample remained $1/2$ to $1/4$ of the U.S. projects (Cusumano 1991, p. 458).

So far, so good. But Cusumano's title conveys an additional message about the Japanese system: *Japan's Software Factories: A Challenge to*

U.S. Management. Cusumano's software factories are revolutionary in the same sense that Henry Ford's assembly line was: Both depended on the interchangeability of parts.

Of course, Japanese programs are not actually interchangeable, but they are built of chunks of programming components, which are designed to be suitable for use in other programs. Cusumano reports that Toshiba's software factory with 2,300 personnel delivered systems in the mid-1980s containing on average nearly 50 percent reused code (Cusumano 1991, p. 218).

According to Cusumano, Hitachi is the leader in this area. In 1969, Hitachi first established a software facility labeled and managed as a factory, calling the facility the Software Works or, more literally, the Software Factory (Cusumano 1991, p. 161). Faced with a shortage of skilled programmers, Hitachi settled on a model of factory division of labor for programming (Cusumano 1991, pp. 161 and 173). By 1988, Hitachi ranked highest among Japan's computer vendors in customer satisfaction with hardware, overall price-performance, and maintenance services for both hardware and software, as well as fixing software defects promptly (Cusumano 1991, p. 162).

Besides the interchangeability of parts, the Japanese software factory model suggests an interchangeability of people. Cusumano himself observed that firms have a natural interest in deskilling programmers (Cusumano 1991, p. 35). According to one industry source, "Only by relinquishing personal control over the deliverable product . . . can individual developers guarantee the integrity of the project they are working on." Within this context, "individual freedom becomes taboo. Some software units depend on others, so the integration of a given new unit into the total release must follow a plan" (Bernstein and Yuhas 1989, pp. 40-1).

Cusumano's picture of the software factory with hundreds of neatly dressed programmers quietly working in their tiny cubbyholes evokes imagery of science fiction. Confining as it may seem, the software factory seems to be a logical extension of the way work is done elsewhere in the advanced market economies. Cusumano cites the work of R. W. Bemer, a General Electric engineer in the mid-1960s, who made numerous proposals to deal with low and variable programmer productivity:

> [A] software factory should be a programming environment residing and controlled by a computer. Program construction, checkout and usage should be done entirely within this environment, and by using the tools contained within the environment. . . . A factory . . . has measures and controls for productivity and quality. Financial records are kept for costing and scheduling. (Bemer 1969, pp. 1626-7; cited in Cusumano 1991, p. 33)

The Japanese model seems to be giving way to a system that offers even more control over software production. With the availability of cheap communication over satellites, multinational companies are finding that they can farm out software to Third World countries where highly educated programmers are willing to work for a pittance. India seems to be the country of choice at this moment. According to Yourdon:

> More important than the claim that India-based software is 30 percent cheaper than American software is the likelihood that it has 10 times fewer bugs and can be maintained 10 times more easily." (Yourdon 1992, p. 16)

Creativity and Control

Japanese programming seems to excel in developing tightly focussed projects with, as I understand them, relatively well understood goals. In such environments, management may be able to structure the production of software so that each programmer works on a small, well-defined subsystem.

When a system becomes so complex that no one manager can comprehend the project in its entirety, highly structured development processes are bound to break down (Gibbs 1994, p. 89). Under such circumstances, the Japanese software factory model just will not work.

The Japanese software factory model has one other critical failing. While the Japanese system might be useful for producing certain kinds of software, it has not succeeded in creating any substantial software innovations. According to a *Business Week* report, industry executives believe that:

> . . . to get the most creative software . . . programmers have to be free to work as they please, beyond the confines of normal business routines. Sun Microsystems' new software subsidiary, Sun Technology Enterprises, Inc., president Eric E. Schmidt says, "Software today is best practiced slightly out of control." (Brandt et al. 1991, p. 100)

Profit-oriented business has never found an adequate system to encourage individual creativity on the part of production workers. Instead, as Cusumano and others have shown, the goal seems to be to deskill programmers, to make them more like interchangeable parts.

Again, we see the liberating potential of information technology giving way to a system designed to keep individuals in check.

5

Panopticism

Smith on Class

While the information age might make analysis of classes more confusing, it also makes such analysis more necessary than ever. To the extent that the information age brings to some enormous wealth, while leaving others behind, it reinforces the class structure of society. Such inequality intensifies class tensions, which, in turn, call for a stronger state in order to preserve the existing class structure.

At the time of the Revolutionary War in the United States, certainly well before anybody's dating of the information age, Adam Smith, the great philosopher of the freedom of the marketplace, anticipated this necessity of growing state power as a result of economic inequality. Smith feared that the working classes were possessed by "passions which prompt [them] to invade property, passions much more steady in their operation, and much more universal in their influence" (Smith 1776, V.i.b.2, p. 709). Consequently, government is necessary to protect the property of the rich (Smith 1776, p. 670ff). Smith even went so far as to teach his students:

> Laws and government may be considered in . . . every case as a combination of the rich to oppress the poor, and preserve to themselves the inequality of the goods which would otherwise be soon destroyed by the attacks of the poor, who if not hindered by the government would soon reduce the others to an equality with themselves by open violence. (Smith 1978, p. 208; see also p. 404)

Smith, however, hoped that conditions would improve. He believed that a market society would naturally become increasingly egalitarian. As a result, he prophesied that over time people would become more accepting of the social order:

> Civil government supposes a certain subordination. But as the necessity of civil government gradually grows up with the acquisition of valuable property, so the principle causes which naturally introduce subordination gradually grow up with the growth of that valuable property. (Smith 1776, V.i.b.3, p. 710)

Here Smith was sadly mistaken about the egalitarian tendencies of markets. Inequality is growing by leaps and bounds. From 1960-1970, the poorest 20 percent of the world's population received 2.3 percent of global GNP; in 1990, 1.3 percent (United Nations Development Programme 1993, p. 27). Today, the world's 358 wealthiest people have assets equal to the combined income of 2.3 billion people, nearly half the global population (United Nations Development Programme 1993, p. 13).

While Smith was far off the mark with respect to egalitarianism, his anticipation that some forces would "naturally introduce subordination" seems to be accurate for the advanced market societies—at least for the time being. Within a larger framework, Smith's vision may be less prescient. The present acceptance of the market may be a reflection of the temporary political reflexes that developed between the end of the Great Depression and the 1970s, a period that did witness a modest move toward egalitarianism. Perhaps in the coming decades the less fortunate will succeed in challenging the great upsurge in inequality.

Based on a worldwide analysis, we find that, in general, where distribution is unequal and the common people become more dissatisfied with the prevailing situation, the struggle over economic resources intensifies (Alesina and Rodrik 1994, p. 485). So far, the forces that support the status quo in the more advanced countries have been able to deflect much of the anger over worsening economic conditions by pointing the finger at scapegoats—immigrants, welfare mothers, etc.

This tactic is unlikely to be effective for long. Accordingly, even more state power will be required. As we shall see, information technologies will be a major factor in both necessitating and facilitating this growth in state power.

Adam Smith deserves considerable credit in partially envisioning the growth of state power. Unfortunately, this element of his work has been altogether forgotten. Instead, his unfortunate legacy seems to be a misplaced faith that the market alone will suffice to cure all ills.

The Panoptic Society

Jeremy Bentham, a contemporary of Adam Smith, provides a convenient symbol of the perverse relationship between modern technology and the diminution of freedom in a market society. Bentham was second to none in advancing the cause of markets. He even chided Adam Smith for insufficient faith in the cause of laissez faire. All the while that Bentham theoretically championed laissez faire in the name of freedom, he was more than willing to trample on the personal freedom of others in his quest to subordinate all aspects of life to the interest of accumulation.

Toward this end, Bentham developed the model of his justly famous Panopticon, a prison from which he hoped to profit from the labors of those confined as criminals or as wards of the state. True, Bentham's object was cruder than keeping people from having access to information. Even so, within the prison, he planned to use his access to information to aid in restricting people's access to everything but work.

Bentham's means were far less sophisticated than what is available to a modern corporation or state. The primitive technologies of the time also limited the scope of Bentham's Panopticon. He merely designed this prison so that an inspector could keep all the inmates in his sight at all times of the day.

Even so, within the small world of Bentham's prison, the scope of control was to be awesome. At every instant, a single pair of eyes would suffice to keep the entire population of inmates in virtual view. Of course, the inspector could not actually inspect every inmate at every moment. To remedy this human defect, the Panopticon was to be lighted so that the observed could not observe the observer. According to Bentham:

> The essence . . . consists in the *centrality* of the inspector's situation, combined with the well-known and most effectual contrivances for *seeing without being seen.* . . . that for the greatest proportion of time possible, each man should actually be under inspection, [but it is also desirable] that the persons to be inspected should always feel themselves as if under inspection [for] the greater chance there is, of a given person's being at a given time actually under inspection, the more strong will be the persuasion—the more intense, if I may say so, the feeling, he has of his being so. (Bentham 1797, p. 44)

What is the relationship between prison life, in which coercion is admittedly a major factor, and a free market in which people voluntarily accept employment? David Gordon recently provided a hint. He published a scatter diagram for the incarceration rate in 1992-1993 and the share of total employees in administrative and managerial positions in 1989 for 10 advanced economies, excluding the United States since its incarceration rate is so extreme. His results were striking.

Canada, Australia, and the United Kingdom form one cluster with both high administration and high incarceration. Japan, the Netherlands, Denmark, Finland, Belgium, Germany, and Sweden form another cluster. Gordon speculates: "Habits of control bred in one social domain spill over to other areas of social life" (Gordon 1996, Figure 5.1 and p. 143). In other words, panopticism seems to be a syndrome that makes itself felt throughout market societies.

Today, a broad array of panoptic agents—both public and private—stand above us. They do not have our interest in mind, but rather prefer to use information to maximize their power or their profits.

Much of this same information has the potential to promote the public good. More than a half century ago under far more primitive conditions than exist today, H. G. Wells realized that such a system of universal information, placed in the right hands, would have a wonderful potential for improving the human situation. He imagined the possibility of a World Brain, observing:

> . . . an immense and ever-increasing wealth of knowledge is scattered about the world today, a wealth of knowledge and suggestion that—systematically ordered and generally disseminated—would probably . . . suffice to solve all the mighty difficulties of our age, but that knowledge is still dispersed, unorganised, impotent. (Wells 1938, p. 67)

While Wells was correct to insist on the potential value of such information, he was sorely mistaken by not taking the nature of the ownership of information into account. Today, this knowledge is no longer so "dispersed, unorganised, impotent." Instead, we confront society today in the form of a configuration of massive databases, whose combined powers are certainly panoptic in scope.

Like the Panopticon, these new databases are thoroughly opaque to the individual under observation. In a sense, in many cases individuals cannot even observe each other without the help of those who own the databases. For example, Steve Case, chief executive officer of America Online, is fond of saying, "Our business is to package our subscribers and sell them back to themselves" (Stahlman 1995, p. 73).

Until this mass of information serves the interests of the great mass of people instead of the narrow interests of corporations or government bodies, this information will prove to be a curse rather than the blessing that Wells envisioned.

Life in the Informational Panopticon

Modern technologies allow panoptic monitoring of virtually all people, not just inmates. Or perhaps more appropriately, we all become inmates in a panoptic society in which both government and powerful corporations are allowed to invade every aspect of our private lives, in the process creating ever more enormous databases that help them to know how to best prey upon our weaknesses.

Given the importance of these databases, we see another reason why privacy is antithetical to market-based information. In such a world, profit is the driving force, and information about people represents a major source of profit. Who you are, what you buy, your tastes, your habits, anything whatsoever about you can assist firms in designing a marketing campaign, evaluating your credit, or making investments in new activities can have considerable value.

Everywhere you go, business and government agencies ask for some personal information. In the process, various levels of government, banks and other financial institutions, health providers, phone companies and even video stores all amass huge amounts of information about each and every one of us. As separate corporations combine with seemingly unrelated businesses, their databases become more complete. In addition, many companies sell their databases to other companies.

As these various sources of information anneal with still other sources of information about you, me, and everybody else, these giant databases give an increasingly complete picture of our daily lives. In other words:

> Through computerized "merge/purge" techniques, companies can produce hybrid lists—for example, of white Democrat male gun owners who have recently moved, or of upper-income NOW members who subscribe to the *National Review*. (Stauber and Rampton 1995, p. 83)

Bill Gates, the head of Microsoft Corporation, a person who has gone to great lengths to protect his own privacy, turns this subject on its head. He predicts a world in which corporations would not assault us with their advertisements and propaganda. Instead, we will program our computers with a profile of our own tastes. The program will then go out on the Web to find the information that we want (Gates 1995, p. 169). He describes this world as "a shopper's heaven" (Gates 1995, p. 158).

While this technology might make a shopper's heaven possible, it is more likely to create a citizen's hell. At the same time that shoppers attempt to express their "heavenly" individuality through distinctive patterns of consumption, capitalism reduces them to arrays of zip codes, social security numbers, and credit card balances.

Metromail Corporation, a leading seller of direct marketing information, maintains a detailed database on more than 90 percent of American households. Hundreds of prison inmates, many of them sex offenders, enter detailed information on computer tapes for Metromail.

One of these inmates, Hal Parfait, serving seven years in Texas for breaking into a woman's house and raping her after threatening to kill her children, used his access to this information to stalk Beverly Dennis by mail. In a suit against the company, she found that Metromail had accumulated more than 900 tidbits of her life going back to 1987. Laid out on 25 closely printed pages of spreadsheets were not only her income, marital status, hobbies, and ailments; but whether she had dentures; the brands of antacid tablets she had taken; and how often she had used room deodorizers, sleeping aids, and hemorrhoid remedies (Bernstein 1997).

Such information is readily available to others besides the inmates who enter the information. A Los Angeles television reporter recently asked Metromail for information on local children, giving her husband's name as Richard Allen Davis, the confessed killer of Polly Klaas, a 12-year-old murdered in1993, whose trial produced a blaze of publicity. Metromail promptly sold her the addresses of 5,500 households with children, along with the names of their parents (The *Economist* 1996b).

The owners of these databases use their information to maintain their hold over the populace, which allows them to accumulate more power and still more information. For the most part, these same databases help to ensure the accumulation of corporate wealth and power in other ways. Take the political arena, for example. Time and again, we have watched while the corporate sector, armed with its financial and informational resources, successfully frames the political debate in order to induce the majority of people to vote against their own interests. When these arm's length methods of collecting information do not suffice and people threaten to resist the corporate agenda, corporations hire spies to infiltrate civic groups in order to collect information and/or manipulate people into embarrassing their cause (Stauber and Rampton 1995, pp. 47-65).

As individuals, we may not feel the direct power of these databases in our daily lives, but that power is there nonetheless. Much that we do depends on our relations with the databases. We have all heard anecdotes about how a simple mistake in one of these databases can throw a person's life into utter chaos.

The Global Panopticon

The idea of Bentham's Panopticon arose in the early days of capitalism, while a small group of people was callously stripping the masses of the people of their rights to work the land. We now refer to this process as primitive accumulation.

The era of primitive accumulation witnessed dramatic events, but they tended to be local in scope. Today, accumulation is occurring on a global scale.

For example, giant international corporations displace people from great stretches of land to facilitate mining or the removal of the trees. Oftentimes these lands are so remote from the centers of production that this seizure seems every bit as distant to people who live near the centers of economic power as the more ancient form of primitive accumulation.

Lacking access to their land, these people must find an alternative means of survival. Many have no choice but to accept demeaning work for a pittance or, even worse, to subject their children to such conditions.

In the United States, the preemption of resources infrequently involves the expropriation of an individual or a small group of people. Instead, public lands are given over to corporate use or, perhaps worse still, the government spends public funds to support the efforts of the corporations, which enjoy de facto control of the land.

Although the confiscation of natural resources retains considerable importance, information is moving closer and closer to the center of the accumulation process. Lacking access to, or property rights for, strategic information, poor people throughout the world cede more and more control to giant corporations. These corporations prospect far flung regions of the world in order to lay claim to patents for the genetic material in the environment and even in the people themselves.

Where can people in the less developed parts of the world turn for protection? In most cases, their governments are willing corporate accomplices. Even if these governments were tempted to help their people, they lack the resources to stand up to the corporations. Unwilling to pay adequate taxes, the giant corporations have left these governments financially weak and dependent on borrowed funds. Those few governments foolhardy enough to stand in the way of the corporate juggernaut must face the full force of the more powerful regimes of the great industrial nations. In this unequal struggle, the rebellious government will almost certainly have to fall in line or give way to a more compliant government.

As a result, few governments will resist the mandate to uphold the status quo. When called upon, they will brutally attack, often with enthusiasm, any of their citizens who demonstrate the capacity to call the international economic order into question.

Attempts by the people to act on their own behalf face almost insurmountable odds. The corporations control the most important channels of communication, limiting people's ability to organize and act in their own best interests.

Should any group earn the disapproval of the giant corporations, the government is expected to use its powers to restore order on the spot. Should it fail to do so, international organizations, such as the World Bank or the International Monetary Fund, or even other governments, will take measures to impose great hardship on the offending agency.

Even if, despite the forces arrayed against them, people could still muster the organizational resources to mount a substantial resistance to this new form of accumulation, the informational resources of the great corporations and their governmental patrons would represent an enormous strategic force. Global communications allow the corporate powers to mobilize their powers instantaneously should they perceive a threat from any quarter. Satellites provide a globally panoptic perspective, providing a view on virtually every square foot of the planet. Security agencies already have the ability to listen in on phone calls and even private conversations.

In a world where information means control, those who lack access to information, or the benefits that such access might offer, often find themselves frustrated and alienated rather than organized. This condition has become especially dangerous now that the procorporate rhetoric has taken the form of blaming all the ills of society on the government. In this environment, some people feel justified in lashing out with random violence, giving the government still more power to collect ever more intrusive information about our lives in the name of fighting terrorism.

Despite the growing importance of information, the system ultimately rests on a material foundation upheld by the threat or the reality of brute force. Such force, like the eye of the panoptic monitor, need not be actualized. As Michel Foucault once noted, "the perfection of power should tend to render its actual exercise unnecessary" (Foucault 1979, p. 201). It is enough that its potential be felt at all times.

Government and the Perversion of Secrecy

The global panopticon perverts the potential of the information economy. While the public provision of information shrinks to open up opportunities for corporations to profit, the public production of secret information grows by leaps and bounds.

Today, with the broad array of intelligence gathering agencies at the federal, state, and even local level, we can only imagine how much additional information our public agencies control.

For example, on the federal level, the Central Intelligence Agency frequently appears in the press. Despite its far-flung activities, the CIA is a relatively small player compared to the less known but far more powerful organizations, such as the National Security Agency. A report by the United States Senate concluded:

> As Director of the CIA, the DCI [Director of Central Intelligence] controls less than 10 percent of the combined national and tactical intelligence efforts. . . . The remainder spent directly by the Department of Defense on intelligence activities in FY 1976 was outside of his fiscal authority. . . . The DCI's influence over how these funds are allocated was limited, in effect, to that of an interested critic. (Bamford 1982, p. 3-4; citing U.S. Senate. 1976. Select Committee on Intelligence, Book I, Foreign and Military Intelligence, p. 333)

The effort to maintain secrecy about our information agencies is so intense that even the size of the budget of the information agencies remains a closely guarded secret.

The veil of secrecy is so strong that it remains virtually immune to the passage of time. The National Archives has estimated it has 300 million to 400 million classified documents dating from the World War I era to the 1950s. Countless other documents are housed in other government agencies (Schiller 1995, p. 49; citing Lewis 1994; see also Smith 1994).

The Department of Energy, which has the responsibility for the production of nuclear weapons, possesses at least thirty-two million pages of secret papers, according to the Secretary of Energy (Schiller 1995, p. 49; citing Broad 1994). Even the Department of the Interior has 30 full time workers to safeguard classified documents (Smith 1994). All in all, the United States government spends nearly $16 billion and employs 31,000 full-time workers just to safeguard classified documents.

So we have the curious spectacle of the government claiming that it has insufficient funds to provide the public information, while it collects and protects tons of files and dossiers that serve no positive purpose, except from the perspective of those who reside at the very top of our social pyramid.

Of course, we can appreciate some types of government secrecy. None of us wants to see the technology for the production of weapons of mass destruction falling into the wrong hands. Unfortunately, much of this information is already widely known, making the attempt at secrecy unnecessary.

Advanced Accumulation

One of the major features of the modern informational economy is a centralization of access to information. This centralization reflects a larger process of centralization whereby corporations combine both within and across industries. The resulting megacorporations have accumulated almost unimaginable powers.

Along with governments, these giant corporate powers enjoy panoptic informational resources. Privatization of formerly public information limits access for others. In addition, the combination of withholding, manipulation, and outright censorship of information so distorts the public understanding of the situation that most people lack the capacity to challenge this state of affairs.

This centralization of access to information represents a major component of the overall class struggle. We might call that part of the modern class struggle concerning information "advanced accumulation" to highlight the difference between the current situation and primitive accumulation. True, echoes of primitive accumulation still reverberate as people in areas remote from the centers of capitalist powers see control of their resources slip away to transnational corporations. In the centers of power, however, advanced accumulation takes a different form.

Rather than directly expropriating physical means of production, advanced accumulation is more indirect. It entails the marshalling of public resources to concentrate informational powers in the hands of great corporations or elite individuals. The public resources might be information proper or the means of conveying information, such as the communications spectrum.

We do not hear much of an outcry against advanced accumulation. Unlike the stark case of primitive accumulation where people directly faced their oppressors, few people are even aware of this new method of creating inequality, let alone the stakes in the system of advanced accumulation. High sounding rhetoric about individualism, entrepreneurship, and the other supposed hallmarks of free enterprise further obscure the public's ability to comprehend what advanced accumulation might mean.

Those who market information or informationally intensive products tend to be the ones who benefit from advanced accumulation. Although the public relies on the purveyors of information for information about the information economy, they are naturally reticent about informing the public about the nature of this process. Instead, those who stand to benefit most from advanced accumulation generally take pains to make sure that it takes place out of the public view as much as possible.

Secrecy is often used either to further the cause of advanced accumulation or to shield the guilty from public scrutiny. As a result, we find ourselves in a situation in which what is left of the common individual's hope for a modicum of privacy is fast dissolving. In contrast, the masters of the panopticon enjoy almost unlimited access to information, while their activities remain hidden from public view.

For example, the momentous Telecommunications Act of 1996 passed with virtually no public input, except for computer users who had some concern over censorship. Instead, major corporations hammered out the key provisions among themselves. Of course, the communications companies themselves, which were the most likely sources of information about such legislation, were hardly enthusiastic about informing people about what was at stake.

Given the asymmetric situation in which those who control information have virtually unlimited information about individual people, while they erect dense curtains of secrecy around their own activities, struggles against advanced accumulation are far less straightforward than the earlier resistance against primitive accumulation. At least the peasants knew what they were up against when they protested the theft of the common land.

Herbert Schiller sums up the logic of advanced accumulation, albeit in a rather abstract fashion:

> The rich informational pool derived from governmentally undertaken and financed activity has been an early target for corporate takeover. In the last fifteen years it has been enveloped in market relationships, its contents commercialized, and its disposition privatized. Its widespread general availability, formerly underwritten by public taxation, has been progressively narrowed and subjected to the criterion of ability to pay. (Schiller 1995, p. 47)

The history of the market for satellite images, to be discussed in the next chapter, offers a perfect example of the techniques associated with advanced accumulation. The pharmaceutical industry has also benefitted handsomely from federal largesse. The federal government first uses public resources to develop new pharmaceuticals, then conveys the rights to this new product to a favored corporation, which can charge inordinate amounts for use of this drug. When challenged, the corporation will inevitably respond by claiming the need to recoup to expenses of its research, even though public research frequently forms the foundation for much vaunted intellectual property rights.

In a rather spectacular case, federally funded research was used to map the genetic structure of human beings. Private companies were then permitted to patent these genes. Those that control this valuable information then have the gall to call upon the full powers of the state to protect their intellectual property rights to human genetic material.

The Protection of Informational Property

Adam Smith recognized that the state primarily served to protect property rights. In an egalitarian society, the need for such protection is relatively modest. In contrast, concentrations of wealth call for a strong state to protect that wealth.

With the rise of the information economy, the protection of existing property rights has been extended to include the rights to informational property. The policing of this intellectual property propels modern capitalist police power to unparalleled heights, far beyond what Jeremy Bentham had imagined to be possible.

Consider what this extension of property rights means. We know that property rights require the exclusion of others from accessing property without the consent of the owner. But how do the owners of informational property rights keep others from accessing their information?

In earlier times, people relied on secrecy to maintain their exclusive access to information. Secrecy was not always sufficient to exclude others. With the proper training or just plain luck, attentive people could overhear the speech of another or somehow catch a glimpse of secret material.

The law did not protect secrecy as such. Owners of information had the responsibility to prevent unauthorized access to information in order to maintain secrecy. The state would only intervene if an intruder violated some part of the law unrelated to secrecy, say breaking into somebody's office. The law was unconcerned that the purpose of the break-in was to access secret information.

Today, the power of the state stands behind those who hold informational property in a much more direct fashion. We should not be surprised. We know that exclusion is central to the logic of a society based on private property, but once society begins to treat information as private property we arrive at a slippery slope.

Recently, claims to informational property rights have been expanding by leaps and bounds. At one point, United States courts were holding that corporations could have exclusive rights to something as vague as the look and feel of a computer program. People claim property rights to everything from images, colors, and even a specific number (Garfinkel 1995). In one famous case, a patient found that his doctor had patented genetic material from the patient's own body without informing him. The courts upheld the doctors' rights (Hamilton 1990; and Berlan 1989).

Some examples of intellectual property claims would be humorous if the courts did not take them so seriously. Some lawyers are now suggesting that athletes patent the way that they shoot a basket or catch a pass (Grover 1996). Only after intense public ridicule did the American Society of Composers, Authors and Publishers back off its intended attempt to sue the Girl Scouts for singing songs such as "Row, Row, Row Your Boat" while sitting around campfires (Bumiller 1996; see also *Wall Street Journal* 1996b). On the same day that the Girl Scout article appeared, a Wall Street Journal article reported that the National Basketball Association was engaged in a suit against America Online over the transmission of game scores and statistics from NBA games in progress (*Wall Street Journal* 1996a).

The impulse to make such claims is not necessarily new. Karl Marx claimed that the invention of the windmill caused the emperor, the nobility, and the priests to squabble over who owned the wind (Marx 1977, p. 496). What is new is the degree to which the legal system has sanctioned such demands.

The courts are moving to protect more and more claims of intellectual property, even though the broader circulation of information is better for society as a whole. Although some claims to intellectual property seem ridiculous, the legal system is acting so supportively, in part because the technologies of the information age intensify the difficulty of maintaining exclusive control of information. In other words, the same technologies that facilitate the initial accumulation of information can also be applied by others who would like to get access to that information.

To make matters worse, because of the peculiar nature of information, protection of the commodity status of information requires more intrusive protection of property rights than other commodities do. If I take a can of soup from the store without paying for it, security guards may catch me in the act. The physical aspects of the acquisition of information are more ambiguous. As a result, zealous protection of informational property rights to information requires invasive monitoring. In effect, the protection of informational property rights often requires personal information about those who might want unauthorized access to that information.

We can be certain that the police powers of the information economy will be stronger than anything we have yet experienced. Consequently, we can assert that, given the class structure of our economy with its highly unequal division of property, including intellectual property, the information technologies, which have an enormous potential to expand our freedom, will be applied in ways that seriously diminish our actual freedoms.

Here we encounter two of the many paradoxes of the information age. First, exclusive access to information becomes a major source of private power although it undermines the ability of society to benefit from information. Second, as we shall see, protecting these claims to intellectual property has profoundly negative consequences for the rights of the individual.

Chain Gangs and Cat Litter

Kenneth Arrow recently noted:

> The information base embedded in production workers, managers, and technical personnel is an important part of the market's valuation of the capital of a firm. An extreme case is the valuation of computer software firms, some of which have become giants comparable to large industrial organization, at least as measured by the stock markets. Essentially, their physical assets and indeed their marginal cost of production are trivial. Their expenditures are for acquisition of information, but much of this information is held essentially in the minds of their employees. It has to be asked why the forces of competition do not erode the profits and therefore the value of these firms. (Arrow 1996, p. 126)

Arrow continued with the observation that treating "embedded information . . . [as] capital depends on slow mobility of information-rich labor" (Arrow 1996, p. 127). Why, then, should labor be slow to take its information to the highest bidder? Should we not applaud workers who act according to the much-vaunted logic of profit maximization?

The answer is that corporations mobilize all the powers at their disposal to limit what workers can do with their information. In effect, the granting of property rights to information means that the corporations need to control the people in whose brains that information resides.

Consider the case of Petr Taborsky, an undergraduate college student in chemistry and biology, who took a job as a laboratory assistant at the University of South Florida College of Engineering in 1987. The lab employed him to do testing for a project studying methods to make sewage treatment cheaper and more efficient (*New York Times* 1996).

On his own, Mr. Taborsky discovered a way to turn a clay-like compound, similar to cat litter, into a reusable cleanser of sewage, a process that has many potentially valuable applications. He said that he made his discovery after the project had ended and that he did not conduct any of his experiments as part of his job.

The project's principal investigator, Robert P. Carnahan, maintains that Mr. Taborsky was part of a research team and that the discovery stemmed from the team's decisions. The university said the sponsor of the project, a subsidiary of Florida Progress, a utility holding company, had all rights to the research.

A jury convicted Mr. Taborsky of grand theft of trade secrets in 1990. He was sentenced to a year's house arrest, a suspended prison term of 3 $1/2$ years and probation for $11 1/2$ years, as well as 500 hours of community service. Mr. Taborsky violated the terms of his sentence when he obtained three patents related to the research. He was assigned to chain gang duty for two months, although he was transferred later to a work-release center in Tampa.

The litigation continues. Mr. Taborsky still faces civil and criminal charges. In addition, the ownership of the three patents is still in dispute.

This case has ominous overtones. The university seems to accept that Mr. Taborsky made the discovery on his own. If he had done so at the behest of the project management, his employers would have ample documentation to invalidate Mr. Taborsky's claim to intellectual property. In addition, had Mr. Taborsky's employers been aware of any great expertise on his part, they probably would have paid him more than his minimal salary of eight dollars per hour.

The case seems to revolve around the question of who owns the rights to Mr. Taborsky's brain. I suspect that Mr. Taborsky would not have taken an interest in the subject of his discovery had he never been employed by the university. Even so, if Mr. Taborsky had made the discovery on his own, after he ceased working for the project, then his claim would seem to be on solid ground.

How then can employers defend their rights to intellectual property unless they have access to the brains of their employees even after their employment has ended? So here we have a clever student condemned to laboring on a chain gang over a dispute about the inner workings of his brain. The possibilities for panoptic intrusion are limitless.

We Own Your Brain; We Own Your Life

Consider the case of Evan Brown, who worked for DSC Communications, Inc. of Plano, Texas. Mr. Brown was not involved in any research project. The company employed him to maintain a computer system for engineers who design cellular-phone switches.

On his own, he discovered a way to regenerate the original code of a computer program so that the old programs could be translated into modern software languages. The idea is far afield from DSC's traditional business, but it could be worth a considerable amount of money.

The company fired him and is suing him, demanding that he turn over his idea. The company claims it owns Mr. Brown's musings as well as his work (Ramstad 1997).

In another notable case, IBM fired an employee, sales manager Virginia Rulon-Miller, for dating someone who worked for a competitor (Rulon-Miller v. International Business Machines 1985). At the time, the courts found in favor of the employee, but that decision is more than a decade old. Today, the courts are far more sympathetic to the actions of business. Had she been a scientific worker, the temptation to terminate her would be even greater.

Unless corporations have full control over the brains of their employees, how can they protect the corporate cache of intellectual property? How can they ensure that information from the brains of their employees does not drift into the brains of unauthorized persons?

But wait! Remember the claims of Nelson and Winter that firms are the repositories of knowledge. How could the defection of a mere human being threaten the economic welfare of a firm?

6

Information as a Commodity and Other Economic Metaphors

Despite all the talk of an information economy, most economists have failed to recognize how much the ground has been changing under their feet. In addressing the information revolution, we will see that economic theory suffers from the same sort of confusions that are implicit in the misleading metaphor of the information superhighway, which suggests that information is trucked about like so much soap or canned soup.

The problem is that modern economists have traditionally seen their discipline as the science of allocating scarce resources (see Robbins 1969, p. 16). This approach seemed consistent with their well-established practice of restricting their conception of scarce resources to three seemingly well-understood entities: land, labor, and capital.

Economists presumed that markets could somehow measure each of these resources in an unambiguous way in order to ensure that each was put to the most effective possible use. The simplicity of this approach became less meaningful with each passing day as economists' conception of scarce resources became increasingly nebulous.

For example, economists once regarded labor as nothing more than a set of interchangeable tools. In part, this approach reflected a commonly accepted outlook—at least among those who did not have to work for a wage—that labor was nothing more than an almost mechanical capacity to do work. Our common language crystallized this perception, casually referring to workers as hired hands.

Happily, most economists have abandoned this dehumanized perspective, realizing that workers are heterogeneous. This evolution reflected the changing circumstances of economists themselves. In the early days of economics, no major economist, with the possible exception of Thomas Robert Malthus, worked for a wage. Over time, as more economists became dependent on salaries, economists no longer believed that all wageworkers were merely brute instruments of labor.

In order to come to grips with this expanded vision of the labor force, economists devised a new concept. Specifically, they invented a new resource, which they called, "human capital," a theoretical quantity, which is supposed to reflect the effect of the education and experience of a worker. Thus, human capital is separate from and in addition to the conception of the worker as a basic mechanical device.

You may find the idea of human capital to be a bit weird. I do. Certainly, the language is wonderfully ambiguous, mixing the idea of "human" with capital—an obviously inhuman concept. According to the imagery of human capital, we have a mix of the "human" aspect of labor—which, ironically, is comparable to the earlier inhuman vision of labor as a pair of hands or arms—together with an inhuman or capital part—reflecting education and experience, aspects of life that we normally associate with a humanizing influence.

Does the human being somehow give life to the capital? Or perhaps we should say that the concept of human capital dehumanizes humans to the level of capital. In order to be fully human, a person must enjoy ownership of a significant quantity of this particular form of capital.

For the rest of humanity, they will function best as unthinking machines. For example, according to a statement from a 1995 roundtable of the Fraser Institute, a conservative Canadian think tank: "The most important job skill anyone must learn is 'not being insubordinate'" (Spink 1997, p. 21).

Despite the metaphorical confusion, the theory of human capital does reflect an undeniable truth. Workers' education or experience can often amplify their productivity, even though formal educational qualifications frequently have nothing to do with what workers are expected to do on the job.

What about information? Our language, it seems, is not yet adequate to address the concept of an information economy. Since we recognized that information is both widespread and intangible, we tend to speak of information in metaphorical terms. For example, we often hear of the genetic information that lies at the heart of the simplest biological life forms.

The "information" in the notion of an information economy is different from human capital. We might think of human capital as a particular kind of private information, in which the concept of an information economy mixes together all sorts of information: public information, private information, commercially available information, etc.

While some of the estimates of the contribution of information are excessive, information undeniably plays an increasingly important role in our economy. Unfortunately, economists are ill prepared to deal with the idea of an information economy. Let us see why.

Why Information Should Not Be Treated as a Commodity

Market relationships are particularly inappropriate for handling information. Why should that be? Keep in mind that scarcity is central to the logic of the market. After all, the supposed purpose of property rights is to induce people to economize on scarce resources.

Information is not scarce in the same sense as other commodities are. Kenneth Arrow recently noted, "Patents and copyrights are social innovations designed to create artificial scarcities where none exist naturally" (Arrow 1996, p. 125).

In spite of the efforts to make information artificially scarce, economists realize that information differs from scarce goods, such as detergents or canned soups. In the jargon of economics, information is nonrivalrous. This strange-sounding term is meant to convey a simple, but crucial point. If I eat a can of soup, less soup remains for you. Soup, then, is rivalrous.

Most commodities, as well as most traditional economic activities, are rivalrous. If I'm going to farm a piece of land, then I expect to be able to exclude the rest of the world from disrupting my fields or taking my crops without compensating me. Traditional schoolroom education may also be rivalrous in the sense that the capacity of educational facilities is limited. When a school becomes full, accepting a new student requires the displacement of another.

Information is another case altogether. After all, we do not use up information in the same way that we use up food or fuels. You do not give up possession of information when you sell it to me. If I consume a bit of information, I do not impair your access to information. With information, you *can* have your cake and eat it too.

In short, using the market to exclude people from access to information is self-defeating. It does not increase our information. It only spreads ignorance. In fact, my consumption of information may even add to the pool of social information, possibly creating an advantage for you.

For example, if you let me read your book or use your computer program, you may benefit from my experience. In fact, unlike rivalrous goods, which can be used up, the more that people partake of the supply of information, the greater the total stock of information becomes. In short, using information can spawn more and better information. For example, as a scientist learns more about her field, she has more to share with others. While scientists might compete with each other for the priority of a finding, the discovery of one enriches all.

As a result, the fields of research are very different from agricultural fields. While exclusivity is imperative in the farmer's field, it makes no sense whatsoever in science. After all, the more information that I gather, the more potential information is available to you.

I cannot emphasize this point enough: The concept of scarcity is absolutely irrelevant to information. The more we restrict other people's access to information, the less we are able to utilize information for our own use. Economics, which economists themselves define as the allocation of scarce resources, has little to offer in an information economy, since information is not scarce, except to the degree that we allow agents to create artificial scarcity through secrecy and property rights. More to the point, as our economy becomes increasingly dependent on information, our traditional system of property rights applied to information becomes a costly fetter on our development.

Whoops. Economics Doesn't Work Anymore

As I just mentioned, the concept of rivalrous goods is central to the theory of market economics. The market is supposed to work because it sets a price on a good that excludes all but those who can afford to get the most use from that good.

But excluding people from information does us no good whatsoever. As a result, our basic concepts of economics are of no use in an information economy, except in one paradoxical sense.

The fundamental theorem of economics concludes that goods should be priced at their marginal cost—the cost of producing one more unit of production. All those who are unwilling or unable to pay that price should be excluded from using that good.

Kenneth Arrow observed that in the case of information, even though the original cost of gathering the information may have been substantial, the cost of transmitting this information on to others is minimal (Arrow 1962b, pp. 614-6). In other words, the marginal cost of information is effectively zero. For example, the discovery of an important natural law may be a heroic event, yet the cost of sharing it with the rest of the world is insignificant. A scientist could simply post it on the Internet for all to read.

Here we come to our paradox of the economics of the information economy: Even though economic theory is severely biased toward markets, according to the criteria of economics, information should not be treated as private property. As a result, when information becomes the dominant resource, the laws of economics tell us that the laws of economics themselves are invalid, since information should not be priced as a scarce resource.

Arrow pointed to still another flaw inherent in the market for information that further undermines the case for a market in information. Markets need informed customers. In this sense, information is different from other goods. In shopping for clothing, for example, we can get information about the clothing by browsing through the store. We can even try on an article of clothing to see how it looks or feels. In the case of information, by contrast, the information about the product and the product itself are identical. We can possess an informational product merely by learning about it. Consequently, the owner strives to keep the information as secret as possible, preventing us from shopping for information in an informed manner (Arrow 1962b, p. 615). As a result, an informed market in information is a contradiction in terms.

Arrow's logic is indisputable. To begin with, since the marginal cost of information is zero, information should be free. Besides, even if we want to work within a market system, the market cannot work well because people cannot know the value of the information that they contemplate buying without first acquiring that information.

In the absence of markets for information, who would create the supply of information? Here we are on less firm ground. We know that, in a market society, few people would be willing to devote much time and energy to producing a product that was free for the taking, unless a supplementary return, such as advertising, subsidized the product.

So we can see why Robert Merges concluded that "patents (and perhaps intellectual property generally) were born as a response to market failure" (Merges 1995, p. 104). Markets still fail. Unregulated markets for information just will not work for the reasons that we have just discussed.

The Economics of Public Goods

Who, then, should pay for the production of information in a rationally organized economy? Here we can turn to the study of economics for some guidance. According to conventional economic theory, goods with zero marginal costs should be public goods to be given away without cost rather than be sold as a commodity. In fact, conventional economics tells us that public goods are poor candidates for commodity status.

In the case of public goods, the best arrangement is to have the government pay for their production with what are called lump-sum taxes—taxes that are imposed on people regardless of whether they use the commodity or not. Is that arrangement fair? Surprisingly, almost all economists agree with this line of reasoning, although some who are particularly antagonistic to government policies in an effort to try to devise ways to turn public goods into private goods.

Those accustomed to the logic and the discipline of the market might ask why should the government pay to produce a good that it then gives away? Shouldn't the government at least charge a user fee?

No. Economics teaches that goods are supposed to be priced at their marginal cost. If the state collected a tax or user fee each time a person used a unit of information, the tax would be inefficient in the same way that charging prices for public goods are inefficient. Charging a fee would discourage the use of information even though such usage would impose no cost on the rest of society.

Imagine a government that had a reservoir of information. Remember that markets are supposed to work because they encourage people to economize on scarce resources, such as food or fuel. Such economization, in turn, is supposedly beneficial because it induces people to conserve scarce resources, but we have no reason to want people to conserve information. The pool of information is not scarce. Rationing it would serve no purpose.

Once the government possessed that information, distributing it would not cost anything. As a result, the government could provide a benefit to many people at no cost whatsoever.

You might expect that the idea of public goods would seem terribly threatening to the powers that be. In fact, the theory of public goods slips through most textbooks virtually unnoticed. When students read about public goods in their textbooks, they usually find obscure examples, such as national defense or lighthouses, rather than items that play an unimportant role in our daily lives. Few economists have noticed that the rise of an information economy is thrusting the theory of public goods onto center stage.

Of course, the production of public goods consumes resources. Society will still have to decide which public goods it will produce, but the market is ill suited to such a task. Let us take the example of a movie—admittedly a good with a typically low informational content. The production costs alone of film may run from $10 million to $200 million, but the cost of showing you the film—the marginal cost of admitting you to an already scheduled screening of the film—is virtually zero, especially if some of the seats are empty. Your attendance may create some nominal costs, perhaps by spilling your popcorn, but you will certainly not create costs anywhere near the typical price of a ticket to the movie.

Society can put its resources into producing a movie or a school. Suppose we were to offer children the choice of allocating funds for attending a schlock film or an excellent school. How many would opt for the school? Even so, many of us would be skeptical that market outcomes would indicate what is best for society.

We should also note that shifting informational commodities to a public goods status might actually save money. For many informational goods—say a long-distance phone call—the greatest cost of the transaction involves charging you for the call, which itself costs the phone company virtually nothing (Brody 1995, p. 30). Even in the movie theater, the selling and tearing of the tickets probably represents one of the larger costs imposed by your attendance.

Merely declaring informational goods to be public goods does not solve all economic problems. Society will still have to decide how much of its resources will be devoted to opening new theaters, making new films, or adding new long-distance capacity. We will somehow have to develop new institutions for making such decisions. Perhaps most of all, we will have to raise the level of education so that we will be prepared to make such decisions in an intelligent manner.

Privatization of Information

Unfortunately, economic theory and reality are moving in two different directions. Even though the cost of producing information is falling, information as a whole is becoming ever more expensive. Identifying the cause of the rising cost of information is simple: Information is becoming less, not more, of a public good in our economy. In the telling expression of Vincent Mosco, we are evolving from a paper society to what he calls a "pay-per" society, alluding to the increasingly common practice of selling information (Mosco 1988). Information, which libraries and government agencies once distributed freely, is increasingly becoming privatized (Schiller and Schiller 1988; Schiller 1984, pp. 102-3). In the words of Herbert Schiller:

> The role of the Federal Depository Library Program in collecting and circulating government publications is being undermined by the

> unavailability of those documents. Budgetary constraints have pre-
> vented it from acquiring the latest electronic equipment for informa-
> tion delivery. . . . The government has approved pilot programs in
> which private contractors manage the electronic filing, processing and
> dissemination of data that businesses and individuals are required to
> submit to government agencies. . . . In sum, the national information
> supply is an endangered resource. (Schiller 1985)

To make matters worse, the government, after paying for the fixed costs
of gathering information, often permits private agents to treat this information as private property (Schiller 1984, p. 84). According to Herbert
Schiller:

> Commercialization has been rewarding to private information
> providers and to their clients. For the rest of the population, the vast
> majority, the quality and the availability of information leave a lot to
> be desired. In the domain of general governmental information, the
> supply has been curtailed severely. The American Library Association
> notes that "since 1982, one of every four of Government's 16,000 pub-
> lications has been eliminated." (Schiller 1995, p. 49; citing American
> Library Association 1994)

Consider what has happened with the federal provision of satellite images. Prior to 1984 Landsat data were available for approximately the
costs of dissemination. Since then Landsat has been partially privatized.
That is, the government still pays most of the costs of collecting the data,
but EOSAT, a private company owned by General Electric and Hughes,
controls and owns the data. The costs of receiving the data have skyrock-
eted. Landsat "scenes" that once cost a few hundred dollars now cost
nearly $5,000.

Academic use of Landsat data has plummeted, and many local governments and environmental groups can no longer afford to buy the data.
EOSAT has also been criticized for failure to archive data, creating large
gaps in the continuity of Landsat data.

According to Landsat critics, more than half of all EOSAT sales are
now paid for by the federal government, either directly by agency pur-
chases, or indirectly through government contracts or grants. Since Landsat was started in the early 1970s, the federal government has spent an
estimated $4.8 billion on the program (research and development, con-
struction, launch and operation of Landsats 1-6). EOSAT, which received
a monopoly on Landsat data rights in 1984 for nothing, has reportedly
contributed less than $50 million to the system (due to cost overruns on
Landsat 6).

Here we have the government spending literally billions of dollars to develop a technology. It then offers the product of this technology to a variety of users at a modest price to nurture a demand. Finally, it declares the technology to be mature and no longer in need of public assistance, which then permits the government to give away this technology to a firm, which can then charge whatever the market will bear.

This practice violates the norms of both efficiency and equity. It reinforces the division of society into informational haves and have-nots while it provides a windfall for those who need it the least.

The Cost of Creating Barriers to Information

In order that information circulates as a commodity, the putative owner of the information must take positive steps to exclude other members of the community from accessing the information without permission. The origins of the cable television industry nicely illustrate this point.

The concept of cable television arose from the experience of isolated communities that had no local television stations. These communities constructed large antennae, which were capable of receiving more distant transmissions. They then rebroadcast the television signals to the community at large.

Soon cable companies realized this activity as a source of profit, but with a major modification. Rather than rebroadcasting the signal to the entire community, they strung cables to carry the programming. These cables represent the major cost of their industry. However, the purpose of the cables was not to deliver the product, but rather to exclude everybody who did not pay the cable operator for receiving the same signal, which could be inexpensively retransmitted by the community.

Cable companies routinely refused to string their cables anywhere except fairly densely populated areas. Customers on the fringes were left without service until expensive satellite dishes came on the market. To make sure that their customers do not take "too much" of their product, the cable companies, who also control most of the material available from the satellites, installed expensive scrambling devises and descramblers so that they can degrade the signal for the satellite dish owners who do not pay for premium service.

Cable companies also incur significant costs by billing customers and connecting and disconnecting their service. Such activities do nothing to improve the service of cable companies. Today, cable companies are so profitable that they are selling for several thousand dollars per customer even though the marginal cost of their services is trivial. In short, the cable industry has spent an enormous amount of funds to convert an inexpensive public service into an expensive commodity.

Today, cable systems are laying new and improved cables that can add to the value of their product, say by connecting customers to the Internet. The industry never foresaw that the cables, which they originally intended merely to restrict access, could serve a positive purpose. The industry just happened upon these new uses by accident.

This unforeseen result should in no way justify the conversion of cable signals into commodities. After all, if the common application of burglar alarms turned out to serve some purpose other than protecting property from thieves, we should not credit those who threaten to rob us with providing a useful service.

The Restriction of the Supply of Information

The restriction of information is not unique to the cable companies. All profit maximizing corporations that market information have two different reasons to make information scarce. To begin with, just as is the case for any other commodity, restricting the supply can make potential customers willing to pay more.

Of course, where competition is strong, when one firm restricts the supply, others might rush in to fill the gap. Competition, however, is not nearly as effective as the business world would lead us to believe. Powerful firms always attempt to collude or to engineer corporate consolidations with their equals in order to take the edge off competitive forces, thereby hoping to be freer to charge what the market might bear.

In the early years of the twentieth century, in the wake of the first wave of corporate consolidations, that wonderful iconoclast among economists, Thorstein Veblen, after taking note of the ability of the corporate sector to limit supplies, proposed that corporations have a far more powerful interest in "sabotage" rather than efficient production:

> Manoeuvres of restriction, delay, and hindrance have a large share in the ordinary conduct of business. . . . A businesslike control of the rate and volume of output is indispensable for keeping up a profitable market, and a profitable market is the first and unremitting condition of prosperity in any community whose industry is owned and managed by businessmen. (Veblen 1921, pp. 3 and 8)

Veblen's pessimistic vision might well soon be reconfirmed in the information-producing sector. Today, perhaps no area of the economy is experiencing a greater flurry of consolidations and mergers than in the telecommunications industry, which lies at the heart of the information economy.

Ben Bagdikian, former dean of the School of Journalism at the University of California, Berkeley, wistfully noted:

> At the end of World War II . . . more than 80 percent of all daily newspapers in the United States were independently owned, but by 1986 the proportion was almost reversed: 72 percent were owned by outside corporations and fifteen of those corporations had most of the business. . . . Today, despite 25,000 media outlets in the United States, twenty-nine corporations control most of the business in daily newspaper, magazines, television, books and motion pictures. (Bagdikian 1992, p. 4)

Sadly, Bagdikian's evaluation of the media scene is woefully outdated. Since he made his calculations, the permissive atmosphere of the Telecommunications Act of 1996 unleashed an even more frenzied merger wave. Today, we find the same media giants wherever we look: print journalism, broadcast journalism, entertainment, book publishing, cable networks. Before this act began to have an effect on the industry, Mark Crispin Miller prepared a four page centerfold for *The Nation* (3 June 1996) laying out the vast holdings of General Electric, Westinghouse, Time Warner, and Disney. Although the last two are predominately focussed on entertainment, telecommunications and entertainment are a sideline for the first two. In fact, Miller points out that General Electric is ranked number one in the Forbes 500 along with General Motors.

TCI Chairman John Malone has stated:

> Two or three companies will eventually dominate the delivery of telecommunications services over information superhighways worldwide. The big bubbles get bigger and the little bubbles disappear. (Grossman 1995, pp. 173-4; citing Halonen 1994, p. 31)

In the future, will three or four giant telecommunications firms compete any more vigorously than the big three automotive makers did in the 1950s and 1960s? The automobile companies at least eventually had to face up to international competition. The large information industries are already global in scope. From where would their potential challengers come?

At this point, we should turn to the second reason to restrict information. Providers of information are naturally reticent to supply any information that would place their own operations in a bad light. In the case of those providers who depend on advertising, we would have to extend this reluctance to supply information to include a concern for the sensitivities of those who pay for advertisements. As a result, critical information rarely surfaces from the corporate sector.

Today, a media giant such as General Electric, whose tentacles spread out into almost every sector of the economy, would be unlikely to develop and circulate information that would threaten any one of its holdings. For example, with the two largest suppliers of nuclear power controlling two of the three major television networks, we cannot expect to see many exposés of the nuclear power industry on our evening news.

In the United States, we have an almost mythological image of a crusading small town newspaper owner. Indeed, we have actually had a few of these courageous newspaper operators among us from time to time. Their operations could survive, even in the face of powerful opposition, because their subscription base, together with a loyal group of local advertisers, could make the paper financially viable.

Today, with the rise in importance of national advertising, the newspaper chains are devouring the small newspapers at breakneck speed. The local newspaper, once a vital source of community information, is now more and more stuffed with feeds from the wire services.

Would we be going too far to suggest that we are witnessing the creation of an information economy without information? At least, we have an absence of the critical information required to make informed political choices about the world around us. Instead of vital information, we get sanitized stories about the personal lives of sports figures, entertainers, criminals, and their victims. Such information may be diverting, but it does little to help us get a handle on our lives.

The Scandal of Scientific Journals

Let us take a simple example that allows us to analyze how the privatization of information hurts us all. Consider the market for scientific journals. Scientists rely on professional journals to keep themselves abreast of new developments in their fields.

Traditionally, universities modestly subsidized scholarly journals as part of their commitment to furthering the overall educational process. With the drastic cuts in state support for education, financially squeezed universities cut subsidies. No longer solvent, journals fell into the hands of great conglomerates.

Suddenly, these journals became a major source of profit. Prices sky-rocketed. Many journals now cost more than $1,000 per year. These prices seem to bear no relationship to the cost of production. Reviewers, and even editors, frequently work without pay. Authors often submit their articles in digital form, saving the publisher much of the cost of type-setting. In addition, journals frequently require a fee from would-be authors just for the privilege of having their work considered for publication.

Even if these journals had been expensive to produce, the conglomerates should have been able to reduce costs relative to the nonprofit universities and professional societies. To begin with, we should not expect to find great managerial efficiency in the nonprofit institutions. In addition, the conglomerates could enjoy economies of scale. For example, in 1975, a study found that the cost of producing a scientific journal by a company already producing 30 journals is 80 percent that of a company producing a single journal. Consequently, the great conglomerates should have been able to lower costs (see Braunstein 1981, p. 19).

For example, in 1991, when Elsevier was about to buy Maxwell's scientific publishing unit, Elsevier was already publishing about 650 journals a year. High-quality scientific journals, which are "must-reads" for their subscribers, typically enjoy profit margins as high as 40 percent (Snoddy 1996). Elsevier's average profit margin was around 30 percent at the time (Hagerty 1991).

With soaring journal costs, the typical university library can afford fewer and fewer journals—especially those that cost more than $1,000 per year. Rising journal costs also force libraries to scrimp on the purchase of books. According to Walter Lippincott, director of the Princeton University Press, "In 1975 a library might spend 70 percent of its annual budget on books and 30 percent on journals. Now those percentages are reversed" (Applebome 1996).

Certainly, this restriction on the supply of information seems inconsistent with the concept of an information age. For the society as a whole, the previous cost of subsidizing professional journals was relatively trivial. After all, if less restrictive access to scientific information would allow for a single, significant scientific discovery, this outcome would pay for the subsidies many times over.

In the Third World the cost of scientific journals is even more prohibitive. Some entire countries can afford only a handful of publications. Researchers in the Third World often cannot publish in scientific journals, because they cannot afford the publication fees that journals charge (Gibbs 1995). As a result, large parts of the world are virtually cut off from much scientific discourse. We all suffer from the lost opportunity to benefit from the full intellectual potential of these scientists, but alas; science must also give way to the dictates of the marketplace.

We have already seen that by the standards of conventional economics, the public sphere should be greatly expanding, at least insofar as the production of information is concerned. Instead, the reality of privatized information represents a major threat to the promise of an information age.

The Annihilation of Public Science

Treating information as a commodity will impede scientific development in other ways. For centuries great scientists and mathematicians have vied with one another to attain glory for their scientific achievements. Fame and recognition, especially among their peers, constituted the major payment for scientific discoveries (Levy 1988). For this reason, scientists attempted to communicate their discoveries whenever possible, at least once they had established the priority of their work (Stephan 1996, pp. 1201-8; and Stephan and Levin 1992, p. 18).

Scientists still had to eat. They obtained support, first from wealthy patrons, then universities, and finally government agencies. Even a few farsighted corporations generously funded pure science, although the most notable of these corporate sources came from industries where serious competition was virtually nonexistent. I am thinking in particular about the contributions coming from Bell Labs and IBM. Most scientific support came from government rather than corporate sources.

The system of public science worked remarkably well over the past centuries. Today, outside of military research, public science is withering for a lack of public funding. Instead, scientists are more and more dependent upon corporate sponsorship. Even within the universities, the government's curtailing of university funding is forcing science to operate increasingly within a competitive, profit-oriented framework.

This seemingly irrational decline in public support of science is not unconnected with the fear that financially healthy universities had become breeding grounds for the sort of critical thought that the corporate and government elites find uncongenial. By cutting off funding for universities, critical thought becomes virtually extinguished within academia— hardly what we would expect in an information age.

In addition, as government support for universities declines, universities are compelled seek out more and more ways of earning money. Some try to profit by cutting costs so that tuition leaves room for a healthy profit margin. For example, University of Phoenix in San Francisco has one thousand of its eighteen thousand students earning their degrees via computer. The school "has no fraternities, dormitories, or football team. . . . [It] doesn't even have a library, just a research desk with a toll-free telephone number." Perhaps more to the point, Herb Schiller noted, "None of Phoenix's 2,100 instructors are tenured or full-time. They are independent contractors paid about $1,000 to $1,200 per course" (Schiller 1995, p. 79; citing Stecklow 1994).

More recently, the university claims to have hired 45 full time faculty members, almost one for every thousand students (Strrosnider 1997); however, the article was unclear about whether these faculty members were actually teaching or whether they were serving in an administrative capacity.

More commonly, universities, especially the more prestigious ones, are becoming beholden to corporate powers for their funding. This phenomenon represents a three-fold windfall for the corporations. First, university research is cheaper than corporate research. The universities supply buildings, libraries, and other facilities, as well as low-waged graduate students. Second, corporate taxes decline in part due to the savings from the subsidization of public research. Finally, and perhaps most important of all, the corporations get to set the national research agenda (Soley 1995).

For example, a university might be leery of hiring a researcher with expertise in the detrimental health effects of smoking if it wants to lure a tobacco firm to subsidize its research. Corporations often impose conditions on the university researchers that allow the firm to squelch any research that leads to unwelcome conclusions (Gibbs 1996). This censorious policy toward the universities extends well beyond the sphere of research. Anybody who questions the corporate agenda poses a risk to the university's finances (Gibbs 1996).

The universities, for their part, in their zeal to tap the commercial potential of their researchers, reconfigure their academic programs. They gladly let the humanities wither in order to build up the prestige of their research arms. The commercial fervor of the universities more or less obliterates any distinction between corporate and university research. Derek Bok, former president of Harvard, in his final President's Report to the university's Board of Overseers, found "the commercialization of universities as (perhaps) the most severe threat facing higher education." He went on to warn:

> [Universities] appear less and less as a charitable institution seeking truth and serving students and more and more as a huge commercial operation that differs from corporations only because there are no

shareholders and no dividends. (Schiller 1995, p. 47; citing McMillen 1991)

According to the University of Miami's vice president for research, "As money becomes less and less available, more people are going to be compromising their principles, compromising their time. . . . We can get to the point at some stage in this process where we're not research universities any longer but fee-for-service corporations—hired guns" (Schiller 1995, p. 47, citing De Palma 1991).

In this world, academic careers rest on the ability to land corporate or government (read: military) contracts. Researchers can either work at the behest of corporate "donors" or attempt to become independent by seeking out profitable discoveries either to patent or to use as the basis for their own firms.

The legal system is bending over to accommodate such practices. Today, a biologist can patent a sequence of genetic material or a mathematician can patent an algorithm. The implications for science are ominous.

Markets, Secrecy, and the Stifling of Science

In the commercial world, unlike the traditional university environment, secrecy is uppermost. The free flow of information threatens to erode profitable opportunities, even though it increases the spread of scientific knowledge.

Of course, if this new system of profit-oriented research provides the incentives for a superior technology that will improve our lives, it might be worth the erosion of intellectual freedom within academia. I doubt that such science will prove to be particularly effective for several reasons.

First, the search for profit is contaminating the entire scientific process. Researchers, who once worked in the open to win recognition from their peers, now shroud their research in secrecy, in the hopes of striking it rich. Such secrecy is antithetical to science.

Firms, too, rely on secrecy in order to reap the exclusive rewards from their activities. Consider the planning of science in the case of the corporations that produce pharmaceuticals. The scientists who investigate the properties of a potential pharmaceutical product often discover that it serves a completely unexpected use. Since labs in the larger firms have more people working on a wider range of projects, they are more likely to find a potential use for any particular chemical. As a result, in this industry the larger firms tend to be more productive (Henderson and Cockburn 1996).

We can think of the large pharmaceutical company as an amalgam of many small companies. This larger group of researchers can afford to communicate since the corporation can reap the rewards of what one scientist learns from another. In this sense, the communication among scientists within the large firm may resemble what science would be like in an open world, but with obvious differences.

In an open world, the cross-fertilization within the large pharmaceutical company would be part of a larger process whereby progress in one industry sparks important innovations in unrelated industries. In fact, many of our great technological achievements occurred because of scientific innovations unexpectedly jumping from one industry to another.

These potential spillovers imply that the more scientists are free to cooperate and collaborate, unrestricted by the need for corporate secrecy, the more society will harvest from the scientific process. Thus, the fragmenting of science into small enclaves ruled by independent corporate powers discourages scientific exchange.

Second, we must recognize that markets are an inappropriate venue for setting scientific priorities. Business is reluctant to fund projects that do not deliver relatively high profits in a short period of time. In addition, business generally makes plans that tightly focus on a narrow commercial endeavor.

Basic scientific research cannot focus in the same way that a business can. Many of the greatest scientific discoveries are serendipitous. A scientific investigation that begins by looking into a specific area of interest frequently leads in unexpected directions. Even though the ultimate result may pay huge dividends in terms of social benefits, business cannot plan for such an outcome. As a result, funding basic research is an unattractive proposition for business.

In addition, most important scientific endeavors require a long gestation period. Even if business could somehow anticipate the outcome of a scientific venture, since it may not pay off for a generation, business, with its eye ever on the next quarterly report, would have little incentive to fund such research.

Here we come to a third problem. We have already noted that when a scientist makes a significant contribution that leads to a commercially viable discovery, the ultimate beneficiary of the discovery may be another firm or even another industry. The employer of the scientist may have difficulty in collecting royalties from firms in the industry that this science has benefitted. Even if the firm is able to collect the royalties, it may have to dissipate huge amounts in legal wrangling about the royalties.

Since those who fund science cannot be assured that they will be able to reap all the rewards from their laboratories, business will invest less in science than would otherwise be the case if society as a whole would make the decision. Economists have long understood that markets lead to less investment in science than would be socially desirable, but they have never been able to figure out a way to avoid this problem within the context of a market economy. With less investment in science, we face widespread unemployment of our scientists.

Thus we find ourselves in a world filled with complexities that call for an acceleration of scientific efforts, at the same time market forces dictate that we cannot afford to employ many of our scientists. This seeming oversupply of scientists should stand as a stunning indictment of our economic system.

Again, maybe this system will prove beneficial for society in the long run; but I see little grounds for optimism in this respect. The commercialization of science may stimulate the practical application of scientific principles in the short run, but it will surely stunt the sort of basic science on which these applications are built.

The flowering of today's commercial successes depends on scientific discoveries from decades ago when science still enjoyed considerable public support. In a major study of recent patent applications, Francis Narin and his colleagues attempted to track down the funding source of the scientific research that the patent applicant cited on the first page of the application.

They found that 73 percent of the main science papers cited by American industrial patents in two recent years were based on domestic and foreign research financed by government or nonprofit agencies. Even International Business Machines—famous for its research prowess and numerous patents—was found to cite its own work only 21 percent of the time (Narin et al., forthcoming).

So, while we may be able to reap the harvest of older science for a while, we need to plant the seeds of future science. Corporations are reluctant to fund any science that does not promise discoveries that pay off almost immediately. Who, then, will fund the pure science upon which our future depends?

The Brave New World of Managed Care

The market is creating a serious deterioration of information in the medical science. Consider the case of the famed Sloan-Kettering hospital, which has long stood at the pinnacle of the fight against cancer. Doctors at this institution have not just treated patients; they have also been responsible for many of the breakthroughs in cancer research.

Alas, the benefits from Sloan-Kettering's research into the improvement of the treatment of cancer did not translate into profit for the hospital. Instead, its research became a public good that benefitted the world as a whole.

Not surprisingly, treatment at Sloan-Kettering has been more expensive than treatment at cut-rate institutions. Insurers, anxious to curtail costs, have been reluctant to send patients there. During the last two years, Sloan-Kettering closed three patient floors totaling 148 beds, or nearly a fourth of its total bed capacity, to cut costs. It has also laid off nurses and paid $8 million in early retirement packages to 164 employees, including doctors and executives (Lagnado 1996).

Recently, the hospital signed a sweeping contract with Empire Blue Cross and Blue Shield, New York's largest health insurer. We can expect more cost-cutting measures to occur. Among the casualties will be the institution's commitment to research. In fact, all teaching hospitals are vulnerable in the increasingly profit-oriented atmosphere of the health care industry. Again, the public needs of scientific progress falls victim to the private profit motive.

In addition, the pharmaceutical industry depends on teaching hospitals to carry out tests of new drugs (Freudenheim 1997). Perhaps even more ominously, because the managed care industry is limiting medical treatment so extensively, the government has decided that the United States is producing too many doctors. As a result, the federal government is now paying 41 of New York's teaching hospitals $400 million to not train as many new doctors (Rosenthal 1997).

Markets and Informational Efficiency

Economics of Information and Trust

Many economists date the beginning of the modern treatment of the economics of information with George Stigler's 1961 article on that subject (Stigler 1961). There, Stigler analyzed the problem of acquiring information about different dealers' offers for a product, which might differ in quality or the services that the dealer provides.

This insight was by no means novel. We can read in John Stuart Mill's *Principles:*

> Not only are there in every large town, and in almost every trade, cheap shops and dear shops, but the same shop often sells the same article at different prices to different customers: and, as a general rule, each retailer adapts his scale of prices to the class of customers whom he expects. (Mill 1848, p. 242)

Stigler went one small step further than Mill. He noted that the customer must compare the savings from searching out additional information about the market with the expense in gathering that information.

Stigler neglected one aspect of this information gathering process: trust. How much can you trust the dealer's assurance about the quality of the good or future service? Consider the treatment of trust by Alfred Marshall, perhaps the most influential economist of the early twentieth century, concerning the economics of information:

> A producer, a wholesale dealer, or a shopkeeper who has built up a strong connection among purchasers of his goods, has a valuable property. . . . [He] expects to sell easily to them because they know and trust him and he does not sell at too low prices in order to call attention to his business, as he often does in a market where he is little known. (Marshall 1923, p. 102)

In effect, then, within the context of Stigler's analysis of information, Marshall was telling his readers that the trust that dealers garner affects the quality of the information that Stigler's customers gather. From this perspective, trust represents an important part of our stock of information, or at least trust is an effective substitute for information.

In another context, Albert Hirschman pointed out that such trust, like information, increases with use (Hirschman 1984, p. 93). The more dealers nurture their reputations, the more effective information buyers will have about the markets that they face.

Kenneth Arrow put the economics of trust in an even broader perspective, observing:

> In the absence of trust it would be very costly to arrange for alternative sanctions and guarantees, and many opportunities for mutually beneficial cooperation would have to be foregone. Banfield has argued that lack of trust is indeed one of the causes of economic underdevelopment. (Arrow 1971; referring to Banfield 1958)

We should note that such trust is far less likely in a rapidly changing society, where culture and tradition count for little. When economic conditions are fluid and people have the chance to make considerable money within a short period of time, they will be more likely to "sell" their reputation for the chance to make a quick killing.

Charles Sabel proposed a somewhat different understanding of trust. For him,

> Trust . . . is like a constitutional, democratic compact which requires of the parties only that they agree to resolve disputes in ways that do not violate their autonomy, and roots this agreement in the citizen's recognition of the connection between the assertion of one's own autonomy and respect for that of others. (Sabel 1993, p. 1143)

Even here, we can discern something akin to information. Sabel's vision of trust still provides information in the sense that it allows people to be able to count on other people in a way that reduces uncertainty.

On Leviathans, Lemons, and Trust

In 1970, George Akerlof published a landmark article on the economics of information (Akerlof 1970). The article bore the strange title, "The Market for 'Lemons': Asymmetrical Information and Market Behavior."

Akerlof, who had spent time in India, was struck by the difficulty of doing business in the Third World, yet his example of lemons indicated that the same problems persisted in the developed countries.

Akerlof's lemons were used cars of dubious quality. The "asymmetrical information" in the title, then, refers to the fact that the seller of the used car knows for sure whether it is a lemon, but the buyer lacks this information.

The buyer is left to infer the motives of the seller. Most buyers wonder, why should someone want to sell a good quality used car? Shouldn't the owner want to keep it so long as it has no problems? The mere fact that the car is on the market suggests that it is a lemon. By this logic, anyone with enough money to avoid buying a used car would do so, dropping the demand for used cars and expanding the demand for new ones.

The missing element in the market for lemons is trust. After all, mistrust is almost synonymous with the popular reputation of used car salesmen. When Richard Nixon ran for governor of California, one of the most effective campaign ads used against him was a picture of the candidate with the question, "Would you buy a used car from this man?"

Since Akerlof's article, economists have published a virtual torrent of works on the subject of asymmetric information. The majority of these have shown, in the spirit of Akerlof's article, how a doubt about the intentions or aptitudes of buyers or borrowers or employees makes markets malfunction.

In a sense, the economics of asymmetric information is not new. More than three centuries ago, at the dawn of our market society, Thomas Hobbes penetrated the essence of this subject, observing,

> [The] force of Words . . . [is] too weak to hold men to the performance of their Covenants; there are in man's nature, but two imaginable helps to strengthen it. And those are either a Feare of the consequence of breaking their word; or a Glory, or Pride in appearing not to need to breake it. (Hobbes 1651, p. 200)

Hobbes seemed to understand that, within the emergent capitalist society of the time, the benefits of glory or pride did not match the opportunity to make a quick buck. He concluded "there must be some coercive Power, to compel men equally to the performance of their Covenants, by terrour of some punishment" (Hobbes 1651, p. 202).

The necessary terror requires a strong state. Without such a power, "there is . . . a perpetuall warre of every man against his neighbour; And therefore everything is his that getteth it and keepeth it by force, which is neither *Propriety* nor *Community*, but *Uncertainty*" (Hobbes 1651, p. 296).

Hobbes clearly understood the relationship between trust, information, and uncertainty. In Marshall's day, Hobbes's skepticism about the possibility of voluntary compliance with contracts might have seemed unduly cynical. Unlike an itinerant peddler, a solid reputation would have considerable value for Marshall's shopkeeper. His customers were probably members of his own community. He and his family would have frequent encounters with them. To earn their enmity would diminish the quality of their lives.

The new amalgam of economics and legal theory teaches that people should subject legal agreements to a market test. If it is cheaper to break a contract than to fulfill it, then one is well advised to do so (Kuttner 1997, pp. 64-5). While this theory makes sense for an individual, it is suicidal for society as a whole. Trust cannot flourish in such an environment.

Robert Putnam provides a suggestive statistic about the breakdown in trust. He reports that the proportion of Americans saying that most people can be trusted fell by more than a third between 1960, when 58 percent chose that alternative, and 1993, when only 37 percent did (Putnam 1995, p. 72). Alas, in our own world of hypercapitalism, Hobbes sounds far more realistic than Marshall's quaint depiction.

Markets and the Generation of Information

A decade and a half before Stigler's article appeared, Friedrick von Hayek developed a highly ideological account of the economics of information. In the course of his critique of Soviet planning, Hayek argued that a planned economy could not be as efficient as a market economy (Kirzner 1988; and Adaman and Devine 1996).

Specifically, Hayek contended that a socialist planner could never command sufficient information to organize an efficient economy. Instead, he insisted, the best way to arrange an economy is to leave it in the hands of independent entrepreneurs. Even though no single entrepreneur can understand the entire economy, he or she can become an expert in a particular market niche.

Over the years, Hayek elaborated his unsympathetic critique of the socialist system until it evolved into the most effective and most sophisticated defense of the market any economist has yet devised. The core of his analysis of the market was a sweeping proposition: The collective information of the entrepreneurs as a whole constitutes a system of "unorganized knowledge," the informational content of which would exceed that of any single individual or organization (Hayek 1945, p. 521). For Hayek, the price system reflects the sum total of this knowledge.

Recall that Wells used adjectives similar to those of Hayek in describing information as "dispersed, unorganized," but Wells appended a third word to his description: "impotent" (Wells 1938, p. 67). Where Wells associated unorganized knowledge with impotence, Hayek taught that this dispersion gave the price system its power, since it provided each dealer all the information required to specialize in a particular trade.

So, rather than calling for a consolidation of information as Wells did, Hayek insisted that the price system itself constituted the optimal means of communicating information. Accordingly, he suggested:

> We might look at the price system as such as a mechanism for communicating information if we want to understand its real function which, of course, it fulfills less perfectly as prices grow more rigid. (Hayek 1945, p. 526)

> In abbreviated form, by a kind of symbol, only the most essential information is passed on and passed on only to those concerned. It is more than a metaphor to describe the price system as a kind of machinery for registering change, or a system of telecommunications which enables individual producers to watch merely the movement of a few pointers, as an engineer might watch the hands of a few dials, in order to adjust their activities to changes of which they may never know more than is reflected in the price movement. (Hayek 1945, p. 527)

Don Lavoie, one of Hayek's most creative followers, describes the role of markets even more eloquently:

> Like verbal conversation, the dialogue of the market depends on the specific give-and-take of interaction, a creative process of interplay in which the knowledge that merges exceeds that of any participants. As with conversation, the communicative power of the marker is not limited to what is explicitly articulated in words or prices but depends upon background understandings shared in a speaking or trading community. (Lavoie 1990, p.78)

So, in Hayek's world, all that is required to run the world efficiently is that we compete with each other solely on the basis of what we read on the dials of the price system. Although he admits that these prices are not perfect (Hayek 1945, p. 527), the are good enough that any government intervention in the economy is unwarranted. Hayek even insists that the existence of "unorganized knowledge" is so complete that we have no need for the government to collect any economy-wide information (Hayek 1945, p. 524).

Although Hayek eventually won a Nobel prize, largely because of this work, his approach was not entirely new. Earlier, Alfred Marshall had used the corn market in his widely used textbook to illustrate a notion akin to Hayek's unorganized knowledge, writing, "It is not indeed necessary for our argument that any dealers should have a thorough knowledge of the circumstances of the market" (Marshall 1920, p. 334).

Hayek in Perspective

Even those who do not share Hayek's politics can admire his intelligence and wide ranging scholarship. In addition, Hayek had the good sense to reject the approach of traditional economics, which assumes that markets automatically arrive at an equilibrium solution. He eschewed the typical economist's reliance on complex mathematical models. Instead, he concentrated on the ways that market processes develop information, which allows the economy to prosper. Even so, Hayek's theory suffers from serious defects.

To begin with, Hayek takes an important insight and pushes it to outlandish proportions. Compare Hayek's presentation of the price system with that of Douglass North, another Nobel prize laureate. North observed:

> Information costs are reduced by the existence of large numbers of buyers and sellers. Under these conditions, prices embody the same information that would require large search costs by individual buyers and sellers in the absence of an organized market. (North 1981, p. 36)

In other words, for North, in such an environment prices will be readily available. People will not have to go to great lengths to compare prices, providing a measure of convenience. In contrast, Hayek proposes that the price system forms an analog of Wells's World Brain.

How much information do prices really offer? Even before Hayek, many critics had already pointed out that prices could only reflect partial information.

Indeed, many of the most important aspects of our existence fall outside the price equation. For example, clean air and safe water are excluded from the balance sheet. In addition, the price structure has no way of adequately taking the future into account. Hayek's theory is better suited to understanding the role of the future than is conventional economics, but it too falls woefully short.

The most egregious error of Hayek's theory of information consists in his naive faith that prices necessarily convey real information. All too often, prices reflect what we will call later in this chapter "pseudo-information." Hayek ignores all shortcomings of the market. Instead, following Adam Smith's two-centuries-old metaphor of the invisible hand, Hayek blissfully presumes that the price system, together with self-interest, necessarily will lead profit-maximizing firms to act in the public interest.

Notwithstanding Hayek's faith in the market, prices do not convey information that leads firms to serve social needs. Instead, they create a distorted picture of society to which firms must conform in order to maximize profits. Economists have long known that such distortions can occur, but they refer to these distortions as "externalities." This terminology is important since it reflects economists' conviction that such disturbances are a minor concern rather than a pervasive phenomenon.

Despite his enormous sophistication, Hayek never raised the possibility that the price structure could convey anything but information that would be valuable to society. In reality, because of the shortcomings in the price structure, prices ultimately communicate to firms that they should benefit by imposing costs on the rest of society.

Hayek's Unconscious Concession

These distortions in prices can wreak havoc in an economy, but the economic literature offers few glimpses into the pervasive shortcomings of the market. Despite his unwavering faith in the price system, Hayek himself provides one such clue about how the price system can lead us astray. In his classic, *The Pure Theory of Capital,* he noted that small changes in the interest rate could lead to substantial changes in the organization of production (Hayek 1941, p. 293).

Hayek's observation is extraordinarily important. The same reasoning also holds true, not just for interest rates, but for any price of any input. Even a small error can cause a large response. These changes, in turn, can have enormous ramifications.

Barry Commoner illustrates this point very dramatically with his comparison of the environmental effects of soaps and detergents (Commoner 1981, pp. 153-8). Both products serve similar purposes, yet, according to Commoner, detergents have serious environmental impacts, while soaps are relatively benign. A relatively small cost differential sufficed to make detergents more attractive than soaps, despite the substantial environmental drawbacks of detergents.

Why have most economists before and after Hayek overlooked the fact that small changes in price can lead to dramatically different outcomes? The answer, I suspect, lies in the fact that this phenomenon allows for the economy to behave irrationally—a possibility that most economists exclude from consideration.

Instead, Hayek insists that markets are rational, while government policies are necessarily destructive. Why, then, does Hayek allow interest rates to introduce an element of irrationality? Not being privy to Hayek's motives, I can only make suggestions. First, Hayek took many of his ideas about economic fluctuations from the Swedish economist, Knut Wicksell, who was a social reformer. Wicksell put great emphasis on the banking system's tendency to set interest rates at an improper level. Second, Hayek may well have attributed the irrational interest rates to government regulation rather than to the entrepreneurial instincts of bankers.

In any case, Hayek did not seem to give any indication that he was conceding anything by allowing errors in the interest rate to occur. Nonetheless, these errors can lead otherwise rational employers to employ too much or too little labor. Since the improper interest rate will affect virtually all employers, investing in too many or too few capital goods can lead to periods of heightened economic activity followed by periods of depression.

Hayek's understanding of capital goods prevents him from recognizing the full effect of these economic fluctuations. For Hayek, all capital goods are homogeneous, except that they differ according to whether they are made by direct or roundabout methods. Rather than define the notion of roundaboutness, let me give a simple example. Suppose you want to dig a bunch of holes in the ground. You can approach the task directly by clawing at the soil with your fingers or you can take an indirect approach by first fashioning a shovel.

Hayek seems to give no thought to how roundaboutness affects adjustments after a recession. As a result, we can say that, in the context of this discussion, Hayek's capital goods are homogeneous without qualification. Thus, if capitalists make a mistake, a recession can correct it within a short period of time. In the long run, Hayek thought that the economy would return to the optimal course despite these errors.

Once we allow that capital goods are not homogeneous and that other prices besides the interest rate can induce firms to invest in inappropriate plant and equipment, Hayek's theory seems to undercut the basis of his faith in the price system.

The Lock-In Process

In reality, capital is far from homogeneous. The displacement of soap by detergent suggests that small changes in price can lead to the adoption of an entirely new production method or a new product.

Here we come to a serious problem. Once the economy makes a wrong choice, often it is virtually irreversible. Let me explain. Suppose a small change in prices causes a new industry to displace another one. After a while, society may realize that the resulting problems, such as pollution, outweigh any cost saving. Or alternatively, the price changes that originally caused the establishment of the new industry may have been temporary.

Once prices revert to their initial configuration, a return to the old methods might be uneconomical. Perhaps the industries that initially supplied the old industry have disappeared or the industry has sunk huge investments into the new industry. In such conditions, reestablishing the old methods may no longer be feasible, even though the original establishment of the new industry was a mistake. Economists now refer to the irreversibility of technique as a lock-in phenomenon (Arthur 1989).

For example, widespread use of pesticides a few decades ago was a mistake. If pesticides were to have been used at all, they should have been part of what has been called a "strategy of integrated pest management." This technique combines biological control of pests with selective use of pesticides. Today, unfortunately, integrated pest management is far more expensive than it might have otherwise been because the pesticides have eliminated so many of the beneficial insects that otherwise could have kept the pests in check (Cowan and Gunby 1996).

The most famous example of lock-in is the keyboard for typewriters and computers, although the cause was not a price anomaly, but a technical deficiency. Early typewriters tended to jam up when one keystroke followed another too rapidly. To remedy this problem, the companies designed a keyboard with letters purposely arranged to slow down typing. As typewriter technology improved, August Dvorak proposed a keyboard arrangement to speed up typing.

The Dvorak keyboard has never been widely adapted, although a number of tests have demonstrated its efficiency. It even appears to have the advantage of lessening the danger of carpal tunnel syndrome (David 1985 and Tenenbaum 1996). The cost of converting to the new Dvorak keyboard would include the training of new typists. If a company trained a Dvorak typist, the company had no guarantees that he or she would stay with the firm rather than seek a higher wage elsewhere. What if some typists could not adjust to the new keyboard? Having both traditional and Dvorak keyboards side by side might cause confusion. In short, inertia ruled out the new, but superior technology.

A few defenders of laissez-faire have challenged some of the most famous studies of lock-in. Unlike Hayek, those who challenge the idea of a lock-in do not pretend that capital goods differ only in their degree of roundaboutness. They acknowledge differences in technology. They insist that irrational lock-ins will never occur since they assume that the markets will automatically select the best technology.

Most of the critical response to the theory of lock-in reflects a fear that the theory of lock-in idea might lend justification to government interference in the economy (Jenkins 1996; Liebowitz and Margolis 1990). This consideration has guaranteed a highly critical response to the theory of the lock-in from some quarters.

Presumably with his strong antagonism toward government regulation, Hayek would throw his lot in with those who are skeptical of the idea of a technology lock-in, even though he assumed away the problem in his work by treating all capital, and thus all technology, as virtually identical.

In a sense, Hayek had engaged in a theory of the lock-in. For example, in the debates on economic planning, which led to Hayek's theory, Maurice Dobb criticized Hayek for this particular failure (Adaman and Devine 1996).

Nonetheless, I think that everyone must agree that, when a distorted price signal becomes embodied in an expensive machine or an entire factory, the consequences will be relatively long lasting. At one point, Hayek even noted that "the equipment of a particular firm is always determined by historical accident" (Hayek 1946, p. 101).

At one point, in discussing natural phenomena, such as the formation of galaxies, Hayek seemed to understand that history, including the history of mistakes, matters. He wrote:

> The existence of such structures may in fact depend not only on that environment, but also on the existence in the past of many other environments, indeed on a definite sequence of such environments which have succeeded in that order only once in the history of the universe. (Hayek 1967a, p. 75)

However, neither in his debates over planning nor in his discussion of economic fluctuations did Hayek ever confront the problem of investment in long-lived capital goods. Nobody, to my knowledge, has been able to demonstrate how markets can generate information accurate enough to prevent firms or even entire industries from investing in inappropriate technologies. Hayek, to his credit, unlike many modern economists, never said that markets would virtually instantaneously reach an equilibrium (Hayek 1967a). The likelihood of a long-lasting technological lock-in, however, constitutes a serious problem for anyone who wants to believe that competitive processes by themselves generate adequate information.

The Complexity of Prices

Even if we ignore the lock-in process, Hayek's notion of the price system as a means of communication suffers from a number of problems. To begin with, Hayek never noticed that, rather than serving as a public information signal, large portions of the price system are shrouded in secrecy. After all, as Oskar Morgenstern, an economist from Hayek's own circle, once noted, the listed price often differs from the actual price, which is commonly a closely guarded secret between the buyer and the seller (Morgenstern 1963, p. 19). In addition, sellers oftentimes give their most desirable customers secret rebates (Morgenstern 1963).

If price were the only consideration for a buyer, then prices would not vary from dealer to dealer, as Mill and Stigler noted. Of course, well-informed buyers of iron ore must go well beyond considerations of mere price in finding the best bargain. Hidden within the price may be a number of nonpublic side agreements. As a result, price often conveys a limited amount of information, especially in the case of producers' goods. According to Galbraith, "More often the firm has an infinitely complicated schedule for all of the models, grades, styles, and specifications that comprise its offering. (Galbraith 1967, p. 194)

For example:

> A price of, say, iron ore becomes not merely $4.60 a ton but $4.60 per gross long ton of 2,240 pounds of Mesaba Bessemer containing exactly 51.5% iron and 0.045% phosphorous, with specified premiums for ore with a lower iron content or a higher phosphorous content; samples to be drawn and analyzed by a specified chemist at Cleveland, the cost being divided equally between seller and buyer. (Cox 1946, p. 37)

Even in the case of familiar objects, the interpretation of price is far from straightforward. Take the case of the lowly candy bar. By the late 1950s, the going price was five cents. By 1983, it had risen to thirty-five cents.

The manufacturers did all they could to confuse consumers while they raised the price in a series of small five-cent increments. For example:

> . . . each increase was disguised by making the bar larger at the same time—the size of the bar having been gradually decreased since the time of the last price rise. . . . Moreover manufacturers, one assumes deliberately, make size difficult to assess by making the wrappers larger than the bars inside, and by using a variety of shapes. (Slawson 1981, p. 51)

Thus, prices by themselves give us only partial information. Frequently, in such cases, *"Price does not speak in isolation* but only in contracts that pose hazards and the associated safeguards" (Williamson 1993, p. 105).

As the center of gravity in our economy shifts away from products, such as iron ore, to more complex commodities, such as information, prices will necessarily be an even less appropriate source of guidance. Surely, this assertion will come as no surprise to anybody who has tried to sort through the bewildering array of long distance phone plans.

With the increasing complexity of contracts, we can expect to see the courts called upon more and more to sort out the rights and obligations of the different parties to the contracts. In the process, the state will become ever more intrusive. In this respect, Hobbes's observation about the necessity of "Feare of the consequence of breaking their word" seems to be more fitting than Hayek's utopian understanding of the price system.

Prices and Personal Actions

The price system is not a particularly efficient method of communicating information for another reason—because we often lack adequate information to make an informed decision. Hayek, of course, denied this proposition. He insisted, "It is only through the process of competition that the facts will be discovered" (Hayek 1946, p. 96). He continued:

> The function of competition is . . . to teach us who will serve us well; which grocer or travel agency, which department store or hotel, which doctor or solicitor, we can expect to provide the most satisfactory solution for whatever particular personal problem we may have to face. (Hayek 1946, p. 97)

How, then, are we to know which doctor will "provide the most satisfactory solution?" Suppose a loved one is in need of medical attention. Would you be well advised to shop around to find the cheapest surgeon?

Absolutely not! None of us wants to face the surgical equivalent of one of Akerlof's lemons.

How do we recognize a lemon? The services of the surgeon obviously have far more intangibles than the iron ore that Cox discussed. Few people without medical training have the ability to discern which surgeon is most capable.

So, we are left to rely on the surgeon's reputation within the circle of people who will give us a recommendation, even though these people might be just as ill informed as we are.

People might try another strategy for seeking out the best surgeon. If prices really communicate information, the most expensive surgeon might be the best. Lacking full information about products, such as surgical services, we might think that the surgeon who charges the most must be the best. A low price might indicate a surgical lemon.

This sort of reasoning was fairly common in the software market before some of the industry giants had established their now solid reputations. At the time, Robert Lefkowitz, analyst for Infocorp of Cupertino, California, observed that in the computer industry, "List price is more a statement of position rather than an economic decision" (Ranney 1985). According to another industry source, "It's similar to using a consultant. If you are paying two consultants $2.50 an hour and $1,000 a day respectively, whose advice are you going to trust more?" (Judis 1986).

For example, Philippe Kahn, President and CEO of Borland, after tripling the cost of a piece of software, explained, "The product is so powerful that we were told its low price was hurting its credibility" (Flynn 1987). Similarly, Automated Reasoning Technologies of Eugene, Oregon sold a large collection of templates to run with Lotus 1-2-3. It initially priced its program at $59. Despite good reviews it did not sell well. At $89, sales went up. At $200 it was even more successful. The company concluded, "Setting a price too low can tarnish the image of a product" (Reid and Hume 1988).

Tibor Scitovsky first described a similar phenomenon in 1945. He observed:

> The habit of judging quality by price, however, is not necessarily irrational. It merely implies a belief that price is determined by the competitive interplay of the rational forces of supply and demand. (Scitovsky 1945, p. 100; see also Stiglitz 1987, p. 3)

Scitovsky went beyond this line of thought. He noted,

> The situation is different in markets where new models or new brands are frequently introduced. A new commodity has no traditional price,

no past reputation; its quality, therefore, is likely to be appraised partly or wholly on the basis of its present price. (Scitovsky 1945, p. 101)

More recently, Sanford Grossman tried to cast this attempt to learn from prices in a more abstract form:

[O]ne is learning from prices what other people know, and that information is conceivably useful in formulating one's own tastes. At its simplest, this concerns the direct utility that one will obtain from consumption of a good. For example, if one sees that car X retails for more than car Y, then one may infer that car X is worth more to oneself, because one suspects that others have experience with this car. (Grossman 1981, p. 115)

Here again we encounter the same limitations with the price system. Rather than providing clear signals to guide our behavior, the price system is often a misleading form of communication. We are often left second-guessing the price system rather than following clear and unambiguous directions.

Sherlock Holmes, Dr. Moriarity, and the Price System

Oskar Morgenstern tells a wonderful story that illustrates how such second-guessing can make the price system go haywire:

Sherlock Holmes, pursued by his opponent, Moriarity, leaves London for Dover. The train stops at a station on the way, and he alights there rather than travelling on to Dover. He has seen Moriarity at the railway station, recognizing that he is very clever and expects that Moriarity will take a faster special train in order to catch him in Dover. Holmes' anticipation turns out to be correct. But what if Moriarity had been still more clever, had estimated Holmes' mental abilities better and had foreseen his actions accordingly? Then, obviously, he would have travelled to the intermediate station. Holmes, again, would have had to calculate that, and he himself would have decided to go on to Dover. Whereupon, Moriarity would again have "reacted" differently. Because of so much thinking they might not have been able to act at all or the intellectually weaker of the two would have surrendered to the other in Victoria Station, since the whole flight would have become unnecessary. (Morgenstern 1935, pp. 173-4)

Morgenstern continued, "Always *there is exhibited an endless chain of reciprocally conjectural reactions and counter-reactions. This chain can never be broken*" (Morgenstern 1935, p. 174).

For example, just imagine that the newspaper accidentally reports a small increase in the price of a commodity. I may take this information to be a sign that other speculators are jumping into the market because they have some information concerning a future event. I then make a move on the market in the hopes of sharing in some of their profit.

Other traders see the effect of my actions and might follow suit, leading to a madcap cascade of speculation. For this reason, the information that the price system supposedly conveys can easily become contaminated. We can watch these information cascades in action every time a small bit of information sends the stock market, the bond market, or the foreign exchange market on a wild romp. The consequences of such behavior can be an increase in unemployment and poverty; yet, these price signals represent the basis upon which market fanatics would have us base our lives.

Alasdair MacIntyre referred to this class of problems, such as Holmes and Moriarity faced, as "indefinite reflexivity" (MacIntyre 1984, p. 97). Unlike Morgenstern, he noted a further complication with the price system: Participants will attempt to break the chain of reaction and counteraction by intentional misdirection. In this effort,

> . . . each actor [will endeavor] to maximize the imperfection of the information of certain other actors at the same time as he improves his own. . . . [A] condition of success at misinforming other actors is likely to be the successful production of false impressions in external observers too. . . . But if I am right the conditions of success include the ability to deceive successfully and hence it is the defeated whom we are more likely to be able to understand and it is those who are going to be defeated whose behavior we are more likely to be able to predict. (MacIntyre 1984, pp. 97-8)

Market and the Destruction of Information

Hayek's theory suffers from still another serious deficiency. His understanding of the price system pays no attention whatsoever to the class structure of society. In particular, as Alanson Minkler pointed out, Hayek's system of dispersed knowledge seems only to take account of the entrepreneurs' or perhaps the consumers' information. The dispersed knowledge of workers falls from Hayek's picture altogether.

Although Hayek may correctly reflect management's perspective, his perspective is incomplete, to say the least. As we have already seen, management has made a concerted effort to wrest informational control from workers. Nonetheless, management has only partially succeeded. Given the importance of workers' admittedly diminished dispersed knowledge, management cannot presume to manage effectively from above without taking advantage of workers' knowledge (Minkler 1993). Even so, management resists acknowledging, let alone promoting, the workers' information. We have already taken note of the length to which management will even go to undermine workers' information.

Shoshana Zuboff offers some further insight into this behavior. She describes the experience of a paper mill, where management made information public to take advantage of labor's potential intellectual contribution. Unfortunately, from the perspective of management, the experiment worked all too well. She reports:

> The plant manager hoped that making the information from the Overview System common knowledge would be healthy. Workers could use it to monitor management as well. (Zuboff 1988, p. 346)

> The common knowledge base reduced interpersonal bickering because it gave an objective basis for judgement. (Zuboff 1988, p. 347)

> The same manager was fearful about the divisional information system. "Right now, I have some flexibility in terms of deciding what data they see, when they see it, and how it is presented. If I lose control over that, it is an important piece of my job over which I will have less control." (Zuboff 1988, p. 339]

Naturally, management discontinued this inconvenient information system.

In addition, I should mention that business goes to great lengths to maintain secrecy. As Thorstein Veblen observed many years ago, "Secrecy and mystification may be 'good for trade,' but they are altogether bad for industry. . . . A trade secret is a 'business proposition' and may be profitable to its keeper [but not necessarily for society as a whole]" (Veblen 1923, p. 269). After all, information expands through use, not secrecy.

Finally, firms will act in ways to limit the information available to their competitors, just as students sometimes rip out the critical pages in library books to impede their rivals from studying (Stiglitz 1995, p. 115). This behavior reinforces the tendency of competitive markets to breed secrecy and foster the intentional creation of misinformation.

Hayek never acknowledged that markets could be antithetical to information. He never seemed to realize that corporations attempt to minimize, not foster, workers' information. Nor did he ever seem to take note of the destructive nature of secrecy. For Hayek, what goes on within the firm is of no consequence so far as society is concerned. Thus, he never bothered to address the loss of information associated with trade secrecy. He blithely assumed that all necessary information was revealed in the listed price.

Public Benefits of Private Information

Hayek's idea about the market suffers from a far more serious defect. We should not judge the market by its ability to process existing information without considering how capitalism limits information by keeping it private.

Within Hayek's framework, a market economy, the public only sees information insofar as it appears in the public price structure. For example, suppose that I employ a weather forecaster who is able to learn that the wheat crop next year will be short because of some abnormal weather pattern she alone has been able to foresee. As I bid up the future price of wheat, other speculators, as well as the public at large, can infer that "the market believes" that supply will fall short of demand next year at current prices.

Society cannot reap anywhere near the full benefits of that information. It is too late for the farmers to plant more crops. People whose welfare might depend on the weather do not know whether the price is going up because people may be planning to eat more wheat or because of an impending change in the weather pattern. My private information has allowed me to win over my rivals in the wheat futures market, but little, if any, public benefit will flow from this information.

If prices did fully reveal information, then neither my fellow speculators nor I would employ weather forecasters. As soon as one of my rivals began to bid up the price of a commodity, I would have information as good as he had.

Of course, firms realize that prices alone do not convey anywhere near full information about a market. They go to great lengths in attempts to obtain information about their competitors' strategic plans.

Prices and Uncertainty

Hayek's metaphor of the price system as an array of gauges that provides decision-makers accurate information about economic conditions is clever, but misleading. Even if prices could give us somewhat accurate information about current conditions, as the lock-in phenomenon reminds us, long-term investments will only pay for themselves in the future. Consequently, knowledge about current conditions is insufficient for making a decision about investing in long-lived capital goods. If prices somehow gave us all the information that we needed, then the investment houses would be foolish to pay for their private weather forecasts to give them an edge in their speculation.

So long as future economic conditions remain in doubt, speculators will bid prices up or down. Someone looking at the price structure would have no way to know for certain the relative importance of real economic conditions compared to the influence of speculators.

If speculation were an important factor in setting prices, Hayek's justification of the price system would fall apart. Investors would be frequently misled, causing great economic inefficiency.

We should not be surprised that conservative economists, such as Hayek, typically rule out the possibility that speculation could distort the price system. To support this position, they have invented ingenious arguments to supposedly "prove" that speculation causes price stability rather than instability (Friedman 1953), but the fact remains that speculation is destabilizing. Conservatives generally blame price instability on labor's demands for higher wages and on central bankers who allow money to be loose enough to allow labor to succeed in winning higher wages. Their preferred economic policies keep money tight and wages low.

Rather than seeing a danger of price uncertainty due to speculation, Hayek abhorred the price stability associated with economic planning or even government price controls. Such policies deprived the price system of the flexibility needed to provide necessary information.

In truth, while government-imposed price stability can introduce an element of irrationality, it can also create an atmosphere more conducive to rational decision making. As John Kenneth Galbraith once observed:

> Stable prices reflect, in part, the need for security against price competition. . . . Price stability also serves the purposes of industrial planning. Prices being fixed, they are predictable over a substantial period of time. And since one firm's prices are another's costs so costs are also predictable. Thus on the one hand stable prices facilitate control and minimize the risk of a price collapse that could jeopardize earnings. (Galbraith 1967, p. 194)

In other words, investment depends upon a certain degree of predictability. My firm's investment will depend in part on what we expect to happen in your industry. Your industry's plans, in turn, will have to take some other industries into account. If prices are jumping all over the place, investment decisions become more difficult. Thus, price uncertainty harms business as well as society at large.

Information and the Bond Market

Let us turn to still another problem with Hayek's theory of how prices reveal information. Information is, of course, an important element of all societies, but an obvious complication clouds Hayek's attempt to justify markets on the grounds of their supposed ability to utilize information optimally: Not all markets are alike; nor are the circumstances in which they operate. Different economic conditions can require very different methods of production and, more relevantly, radically different types of organization, which use information in differing ways.

For example, even before Hayek developed his theory, John Maynard Keynes took note of the central role of the bond (Keynes 1927, p. 643). Here is a widely traded financial instrument that has an enormous influence on the economy as a whole.

In an apparently lighthearted scene in the documentary film about Bill Clinton's first presidential race, *The War Room,* Clinton's chief political advisor, James Carville, describes his previous ambition to be reborn as a king or as the Pope. He remarks that, now that he has become wiser, he would rather be reborn as "The Bond Market" because today the bond market reigns supreme.

In today's political environment, no elected leader can afford to defy the bond market. Should anyone try to put legislation in place that would upset the bond market, huge sums of money would flee the land, seeking refuge in other countries with a more congenial bond market. In this sense, the bond market might be the most important market in our economy today.

For Keynes, the bond represented the price of nonliquid assets in general (Keynes 1931, p. 366). Keynes's bond prices set the tone for interest rates. Interest rates, in turn, exert an enormous influence on people deciding whether to build a new house or sink money into a new venture. In fact, many economists (wrongly) believe that interest rates are a primary influence on new investment.

In a sense, bond prices are relatively straightforward. When you buy a bond, you get back the principal plus predetermined dividends, so long as the issuing agency remains solvent. Ordinarily, you may either hold the bond and collect the dividends or sell it.

Given the enormous influence of the bond market, the sort of economic efficiency that Hayek envisioned would be all but impossible with an inadequate informational basis for the bond market. In all fairness, Hayek, unlike many modern economists, did not believe that a market economy could achieve absolute perfection. Even so, an irrational bond market does enormous damage to an economy.

Hayek clearly understood that economic theory would be of little use in getting a handle on such markets. He observed,

> So far as I know, no economist has yet succeeded in using his knowledge of theory to make a fortune by a prediction of future prices. (This applies even to Lord Keynes who is sometimes thought to have done so. But so long as he speculated in the field in which one might have thought that his theoretical knowledge would have helped him, namely in foreign exchange, he lost more than he possessed; and only later, when he turned to speculation in commodities where admittedly his theoretical knowledge was of no use to him, did he succeed in acquiring a substantial fortune.) (Hayek 1967b, p. 262)

Ignoring the relative price movements of different high quality bonds, the "unorganized knowledge" so dear to Hayek is of little value in the bond market unless we torture our definition of unorganized knowledge to imagine bond dealers whose market specific knowledge includes a relatively full understanding of the state of the economy as a whole and its future prospects over the next few decades. To do so would discredit Hayek's theory since that sort of knowledge is exactly the type of information that Hayek insisted would necessarily elude an economic planner.

What advantage, then, would pure traders have over economists, besides being unburdened with unnecessary theory? Just think about the kind of "unorganized knowledge" that bond traders would require. Keep in mind that bond prices vary according to estimates of the future course of the economy over a span of decades.

What sort of traders, then, could bring sufficient knowledge to this market? These traders would have to have good information about all aspects of the economy over the next decades.

The Pseudo-Rationality of Pseudo-Information

In conclusion, we have seen that prices, unfortunately, are dangerously misleading indicators of the social good. No wonder Makato Itoh concluded,

> A market does not directly reveal information about the intentions, desires and values of its participants, but transmits information solely about the outcome of decisions taken in the dark. . . . Information flows are very fragmented, and information-gathering activities are both duplicated and wasteful. (Itoh 1995, p. 123)

Itoh could have gone much further. He could have added that the price system puts a positive economic value on behavior that is socially irresponsible. For example, the profit-maximizing head of a tobacco firm has every reason to want to hook children on nicotine.

Moreover, prices include much pseudo-information. By pseudo-information, I mean that set of information that has relevance only within the context of the price structure.

Let me give a concrete example. When making an important decision, the head of a major corporation will almost certainly take the present or future value of the corporation's stock into account. Yet the stock price has meaning only within the context of the price system.

Nonetheless, society devotes enormous energies to "learning" about the stock market, even though much of this effort is only slightly more scientific than the quest to discover the means to predict future lottery numbers.

Just consider again the explosion in the quantity of transactions in the stock market. In 1960, 766 million shares were traded on the New York Stock Exchange. In 1987, 900 million shares changed hands in the average week. More shares were traded on the lowest volume day in 1987 than in any month in 1960. More shares were traded in the first 15 minutes of 19 and 20 October 1987 than in any week in 1960 (Summers and Summers 1989).

The stock market represents a relatively small share of the entire universe of financial speculation. For example, besides stocks, speculators buy and sell derivative securities, such as stock futures, which provide the rights to buy or sell stocks at a set price at a specified time in the future. Organized markets in such derivative securities did not even exist in 1970. Today, the value of trades in stock futures exceeds that of the trades in stocks themselves. Trade in the New York Stock Exchange averages less than $10 billion per day; government bonds, $25 billion; daily trade in foreign exchange averages more than $25 billion. Trade in index options equals that of stock futures (Summers and Summers 1989).

Other assets let speculators bet on the future price of pork bellies, heating oil, or foreign currencies. Nobody knows how much all these transactions cost. Some indicators do exist for the stock market. For example, the combined receipts of firms on the New York Stock Exchange was $53 billion in 1987—an enormous sum considering that the total income for the entire corporate sector in the United States was only $310.4 billion. Besides these direct costs, corporations whose stock is traded in organized markets devote much time and energy to efforts to influence the markets. For example, chief executive officers of major corporations commonly spend a week or more each quarter just telling their corporate story to security analysts. In addition, both individuals and firms spend a great number of resources monitoring their portfolios, acquiring information about securities or making investment decisions. If these supplementary costs are one-half as much as direct payments to security firms, then the cost of operating the securities markets was greater than $75 billion (Summers and Summers 1989).

What are the benefits that the stock market confers on society as a whole, not just those who profit from the market? We know that the stock market does relatively little to raise money to finance investment. Since most stock market trades merely involve one speculator selling to another, most of the stock market activity merely redistributes wealth from one party to another.

Even if some people could develop information that would provide you with foreknowledge about outcomes on the stock market or at horse races, this information would provide no social advantage. It would merely allow you to prosper at the expense of other people (Hirshleifer 1971). Certainly, channelling a fraction of the resources now devoted to stock market activities to more productive ends could provide considerable benefit to society.

Some formal economic models suggest that the stock market may give a signal to a bank that a particular corporation is a risky borrower, but I remain unconvinced that banks rely on this sort of information very heavily. Instead, the stock market churns out a flood of pseudo-information that has no social benefit.

The rhetoric of an information age conveys a sense of rationality. After all, what can be more rational than to use information? In reality, pseudo-information drives the economy. Since financial calculations are uppermost, stock markets and bond markets, rather than human needs, set our priorities. No political leader dares to defy the sentiments of the market.

Upon reflection, Carville's seemingly lighthearted remark about the bond market reveals a chilling truth about the utter absurdity of the logic of the information age, in which pseudo-information drives out information proper. A bond trader can only be rational within the confines of the bond market. A bond market puts no stock in human sufferings. It totally discounts the importance of cultivating the human potential. Bond traders merely try to get a jump on other bond traders in anticipating the future course of bond prices.

Somehow, we have come to put our faith in the preposterous logic of these financial markets while the environment, which represents true wealth, rapidly degrades.

Adam Smith's Hamburger

Economists base their faith in the rationality of pseudo-information on the simplistic logic of Adam Smith's invisible hand. You may recall Smith's famous assertion:

> It is not from the benevolence of the butcher, the brewer, or the baker that we expect our dinner, but from their regard to their own interest. We address ourselves, not to their humanity but to their self-love, and never talk to them of our own necessities but of their advantages. (Smith 1776, I.ii.2, pp. 26-7)

In a small, self-contained village based on traditional handicrafts, where ownership of capital is relatively equally distributed, Smith's invisible hand might operate relatively efficiently. In a global economy where complex technology is everywhere, the invisible hand is more likely to do harm than good.

Before we fault Smith too much for a naive understanding of the world, we should recognize that his discussion of the butcher turned out, at least in one sense, to be remarkably prescient. What industry, besides perhaps Hollywood, has done more to expand the scope of markets into far flung regions of the world than the fast food industry, best symbolized by the Big Mac? One recent book is devoted to the theme of "The Mc-Donaldization of Society" (Ritzer 1996).

The London magazine, *The Economist,* has even chosen the cost of a Big Mac as a measure of international prices (see Pakko and Pollard 1996). Another study used Big Mac prices to predict movements in the foreign currency markets (Cumby 1996).

But then what does a Big Mac really cost? The fast-food industry is notorious for paying its workers in the United States at or near the lowest legal standard, and then applying its enormous political muscle to keep that standard as low as possible. Here we have an industry that minimizes the human element in work by specifying the preparation of the food down to the tiniest detail. No room for learning by doing here.

In addition, the industry tries to minimize its labor costs by using an enormous quantity of packaging. The production of this stuff requires the destruction of forests and the depletion of our stocks of fossil fuels. In the end, the packaging either ends up as litter and/or trash. This packaging then fills up our landfills as garbage or in our lungs as pollution, if it is incinerated. We might also ask how much the fast food industry contributes to the excessive dependence on the automobile, with its associated costs in terms of death and pollution.

Many of the hamburgers come from cows that graze in recently cleared rain forests, thereby contributing to serious environmental degradation, including global warming. With the increase of global warming, tropical diseases move into more temperate areas. Then we must not forget to factor in the health cost of the high-fat, high-salt diet that the fast-food industry offers.

Only by ignoring these, and many other associated costs, can we calculate that Adam Smith's hamburger is a cheap and rational menu. But then, Professor Smith already told us that the butcher was not acting out of benevolence.

Information and the Environment

Much of the rhetoric of the information age seems to lend support to the notion of informational alchemy, whereby business magically "transforms signals into commodities by processing knowledge" (Castells 1996, p. 172). Alas, despite the obvious usefulness of information, to the best of my knowledge, information cannot yet adequately substitute for food, clothing, or shelter. Nature still remains the foundation of our standard of living.

True, modern informational technology can potentially help to protect our ecological wealth by allowing us to reduce some significant environmental impacts. Today, we can communicate over long distances, eliminating the need to commute. By carefully monitoring production processes, computers can reduce the use of energy or the emission of pollutants.

Unfortunately, the environmental ledger of high technology has two sides. For example, the production of computers entails a significant environmental cost. For example, in the process of making computer chips, workers are exposed to arsine, phosphine, diborane, and chlorine (Hays 1989, p. 64). The occupational illness rate for semiconductor workers is triple that of manufacturing workers as a whole. Electronics workers experience job-related illnesses at twice the general manufacturing rate (Hays 1989, p. 65; citing LaDou 1984).

Comparing both sides of the ledger, what do we find? Toxic emissions are increasing relative to Gross National Product and relative to manufacturing output for the majority of countries. The trends are worse in the poorer countries as toxic industries relocate to those lands (Hettige, Lucas, and Wheeler 1992). We stand by while our forests shrink and our farmlands erode or become covered with pavement. Contaminants continue to pour out into our air and our water.

In the end, we may have to rely on our informational capabilities to save the resources we have left. Before we can begin that process, we have to go well beyond the market for guidance.

Le Roi est le Roi: Free Enterprise and Capital Punishment

Markets teach us to turn a blind eye toward the environmental damage occurring all around us. This defect reflects a far larger problem with markets in our economy.

Today, pseudo-information takes precedence over real information. As a result, unmet social needs press in on us from all sides. Business has no reason to meet these needs unless it can turn a sufficient profit.

Political leaders tell us that we cannot even afford our present level of government spending on social or environmental programs, let alone commit enough funds to address these challenges adequately. So we watch our cities, as well as the global environment, deteriorate. While the situation worsens daily, nobody steps forward to take responsibility for this mess.

In earlier times, a king, or as the French would say, *le roi,* ruled supreme. He could set priorities and spend money in any way that he saw fit, no matter how arbitrary. Today, we have a new *roi*—or we should say, ROI—which commands our life. This new ROI is an acronym for the Return on Investment. This ROI, and this ROI alone, now determines what will or will not be done. Kevin Phillips has summarized this rule of ROI:

> Finance has not simply been spreading into every nook and cranny of economic life: a sizeable portion of the financial sector, electronically liberated from past constraints, has put aside old concerns with funding the nation's long-range industrial future, has divorced itself from the precarious prospects of Americans who toil in factories, fields, or even suburban shopping malls, and is simply feeding wherever it can. (Phillips 1994, p. 81)

The wild expansion of the domain of this new ROI is far from accidental. Powerful interest groups, financed largely by great corporations or those who already have great wealth, have been hard at work reducing the public sphere of activity. This attack on the public sphere has taken several forms. Conservative think tanks dominate the media, spreading the promise of privatization. Sympathetic politicians underfund public activities, undermining the ability of the public sector to provide adequate services, thereby creating an impression of inefficiency. Finally, in the absence of public financing of elections, corporations more and more frequently can openly finance the election of those who favor their interest.

Schools, prisons, roads, sanitation, and just about any other sphere of public activity are on the road to becoming privatized. Public lands are turned over to private interests who see national treasures merely as sources of timber or minerals or a place to graze cattle. Public information is turned over to corporations, who then sell it to the same citizens whose taxes originally paid for developing the data. Someone once posted a message on the Internet that is too poignant to let pass just because I cannot remember the source:

> The United States has become a place where your neighborhood video store is still open at midnight, while the library is closed at noon; where an advertising agency owns more computers and fax machines than it knows what to do with, while teachers have to wait in line to use a school's one functioning copying machine.

The public sphere is subject to the will of the people, albeit only partially and to a diminishing extent. If we do not appreciate our schools or our city council, we have the possibility of voting to replace them. We can still even have some modest influence on the state or federal government.

Corporations, in contrast, are responsible only to their shareholders. Yes, they are subject to the laws of the nation, but more and more corporations can rewrite the laws, often through the agency of compliant politicians, who often allow the corporations themselves to draft the laws that affect them.

The shareholders, to whom the corporations owe their allegiance, single-mindedly seek out the highest ROI. Sometimes a firm can improve its ROI through a new technology or an organizational innovation. More typically these days, corporations seek to inflate their ROI by cutting back. They cut back on wages, pensions, or medical care for their workers. They cut back on measures that will preserve the environment. Through the politicians whom they hold in tow, they cut back taxes.

The ROI flourishes while society decays. Our willingness to cede more and more authority to the corporations is tantamount to demanding, "Off with our heads."

8

Toward a Real Information Age

Just Another Information Revolution

The accumulation of information is hardly revolutionary. Around 300 B.C. the Egyptian city of Alexandria founded a great library. In ten years, the library grew to a size of some 200,000 volumes. In about 250 years, it had reached a size of 700,000 volumes (Gore 1976, pp. 155-7). If we were to credit any time as the period of the true information revolution, we might do well to select the years following the introduction of the printing press. According to Neil Postman,

> Forty years after Gutenberg converted an old winepress into a printing machine with movable type, there were presses in 110 cities in six different countries. Fifty years after the press was invented, more than eight million books had been printed, almost all of them filled with information that had previously been unavailable to the average person. (Postman 1992)

Other less revolutionary innovations also seemed to open up new informational horizons in earlier times. For example, in the sixteenth century, scientists considered the humble pencil to be a technological wonder that allowed naturalists to sketch what they saw in the fields (Petroski 1989, Chapter 5).

Skepticism about the information revolution has history that is just as long and noble. Postman reminded his readers that in *Phaedras,* Plato had Socrates question the value of writing (Postman 1992, p. 3-4). Writing, worried Socrates, would eliminate the need to develop a good memory and would give people a false impression of wisdom.

More recently, T. S. Eliot bemoaned the information revolution in the opening chorus to his play, *The Rock:*

Where is the wisdom we have lost in knowledge?
Where is the knowledge we have lost in information? (Eliot 1934, p. 7)

For all the continuity in the accumulation of information, we do seem to have reached a watershed. Good conservatives, such as Plato or Eliot, seem to have dreaded progress that might undermine traditional authority. Our modern informational technologies seem to pose no such threat. Left with no tradition to weaken, our informational technologies seem sure to make authority stronger than ever.

We Are a Community after All

Although the new informational technologies strengthen the hierarchical powers in our society, hierarchical organization is ill suited to take full advantage of these same technologies. As Shoshana Zuboff wrote, "An information economy requires . . . a new social contract derived from a new moral vision" (Zuboff 1993, p. 13). One could read such words as just so much New Age babble, but to do so would be a mistake. In more concrete terms, Zuboff is telling us that class relations stand in the way of taking advantage of the technological potential of the information age.

How exactly, then, does class stand in the way of taking advantage of the information age? To begin with, a class society sets group against group.

Like it or not, we do live in a community. The more our population grows, the less we can avoid affecting each other. True, the affluent do not have to live cheek to jowl with the downtrodden. They can retreat to the security of walled compounds guarded by private security forces.

Even so, total separation is impossible. When poverty becomes too extreme for the less fortunate, they avenge their condition in many ways. Society can usually thwart clumsy attempts to break out of poverty through illicit means, although some of the poor do manage to advance themselves through crime. Random violence—even though it usually misses the well to do—is harder to contain.

Other, less obvious influences pose a far more ominous threat to the comfortable segments of society. For example, poverty provides an excellent breeding ground for diseases. Today, lethal strains of tuberculosis, resistant to modern antibiotics, are taking hold among the homeless, as well as among those who find their homes in our rapidly expanding houses of correction. Eventually, such plagues will break out of their impoverished confines and unleash themselves on the same people who now resist spending public funds on public health.

Even if the affluent could somehow inoculate themselves against the emerging public health threats, their callous treatment of the poor is foolish, even on the hallowed grounds of fiscal responsibility. To begin with, we all know that prisons are far more expensive than schools. Even if the threat of terrible punishment deterred all potential felons from committing evil deeds, the abandonment of the poor still would not make sense.

Let me explain: Admittedly, all societies have a small number of sociopaths, but most people have a potential to contribute to society as a whole. As high technology becomes the fulcrum of economic competitiveness, the societies that prosper in the future will be those that do the best job of educating their citizens—not just the privileged few, but the great masses of their citizens. Yes, the investment in caring for and educating children today may not repay itself for a decade or more, but it will certainly prove to be a sound investment in the long run.

In short, class systems can be self-defeating. We no longer need large numbers of poor and uneducated workers to do as much grunt work for the elites. Instead, we need a highly educated work force that can discover the best way to utilize our scarce resources.

Information and the Obsolescence of Class

Treating information as private property is self-defeating. Although the lure of profits may induce some individuals to discover new inventions, property relations will surely stunt the overall inventive process. In truth, excluding the masses from information serves no broader purpose whatsoever, except for providing a small group with the lion's share of wealth and perhaps making elites feel superior to the unwashed masses.

The widest possible distribution of information promotes the learning process, which in turn improves both the quality and quantity of information. The improved pool of information will make possible a better life for everybody. Each industry will know about the advances made in all other parts of society.

We need better high school classes and college classes, not social classes. A class structure prevents us from taking advantage of the potential of modern technology. We need to be able to tap the brains of all citizens, not just the privileged few with access to good education.

A class structure degrades the quality as well as the quantity of information. The market system creates incentives to mislead others. The resulting mistrust makes our information less reliable. The ensuing confusion is costly to a society in which information supposedly stands at the center of economic activity. To come anywhere near the promise of an information society, we need to create institutions that foster creativity in an atmosphere of trust and cooperation.

While our new technologies call out for a new form of social organization, as well as a new way of using technology, these new opportunities will not just fall into our laps. People of good will must band together to create this new society. Success will not be easy, but then such struggles can be exhilarating. Even so, we will meet strong resistance from the powers that be. In their hands, the new technologies will make our task all the more difficult.

An Anti-Utopian Disclaimer

I do not in any way underestimate the difficulty in making people behave cooperatively, but I am convinced that an inequitable class structure makes cooperative behavior even more unlikely. Nor do I believe for a moment that merely improving the quality or quantity of information will suddenly make a good life possible for all, but I am certain that an inequitable class structure will prevent us from taking anything near the full advantage of modern information technologies.

While I do not discount the difficulties in taking a new path, I believe that everybody can agree that our current path is taking us in the wrong direction. Even those who are enjoying the most economic success express dissatisfaction with the current state of affairs.

We are experiencing a disastrous deterioration in the quality of our lives. Crime, environmental degradation, and the disappearance of civility are readily apparent. Class distinctions make all of these problems more virulent.

Of course, we cannot wave a magic wand and declare the abolition of classes. Some would have us believe that we can solve our problems by calling for a more authoritarian government to impose greater discipline. Even if we manage to avoid that course, class-consciousness and class behavior are ingrained and will take many decades to undo. Despite the difficulties of making positive changes in our society, given the enormity of the stakes, we should get on with this business as soon as possible.

Bibliography

Adaman, Fikret and Pat Devine. 1996. "The Economic Calculation Debate: Lessons for Socialists." *Cambridge Journal of Economics,* Vol. 20, No. 5 (September): pp. 523-39.

Adams, Richard M. et al. 1995. "Value of Improved Long-Range Weather Information." *Contemporary Economic Policy,* Vol. 12, No. 3 (July): pp. 11-19.

Agrawal, A. 1995. "Dismantling the Divide between Indigenous and Scientific Knowledge." *Development and Change,* Vol. 26, No. 3 (July): pp. 413-40.

Akerlof, George. 1970. "The Market for 'Lemons': Asymmetrical Information and Market Behavior." *Quarterly Journal of Economics,* Vol. 83, No. 3 (August): pp. 488-500.

Alchian, A. 1963. "Reliability of Progress Curves in Airframe Production." *Econometrica,* Vol. 31, No. 4 (October): pp. 679-92.

Alesina, Alberto and Dani Rodrik. 1994. "Distributive Politics and Economic Growth." *Quarterly Journal of Economics,* Vol. 109, No. 2 (May): pp. 465-90.

American Library Association. 1994. *Less Access To Less Information By and About the U.S. Government: XXI. Chronology: January-June.* Bi-annual (June) (Washington: American Library Association).

Anderson, Edgar. 1952. *Plants, Man and Life* (Boston: Little Brown & Co.).

Andrews, Edmund L. 1996. "Don't Go Away Mad, Just Go Away; Can AT&T Be the Nice Guy As It Cuts 40,000 Jobs?" *New York Times* (13 February): p. D1.

Applebome, Peter. 1996. "Profit Squeeze for Publishers Makes Tenure More Elusive for College Teachers." *New York Times* (18 November 18).

Arrow, Kenneth J. 1962a. "The Economic Implications of Learning by Doing." *Review of Economic Studies,* Vol. 29, No. 2 (June): pp. 155-73.

———. 1962b. "Economic Welfare and the Allocation of Resources for Invention." In

Richard R. Nelson (ed.) *The Rate and Direction of Inventive Activity: Economic and Social Factors* (Princeton: Princeton University Press): pp. 609-24.

———. 1971. "Political and Economic Evaluation of Social Effects and Externalities." in M.D. Intriligator, ed. *Frontiers of Quantitative Economics* (Amsterdam: North-Holland): pp. 2-23.

———. 1979. "The Economics of Information." in Dertouzos, M. L. and J. Moses. eds. *The Computer Age: A Twenty-Year View* (Cambridge: MIT Press): pp. 306-17.

———. 1996. "The Economics of Information: An Exposition." *Empirica,* Vol. 23, No. 2, pp. 119-28.

Arthur, W. Brian. 1989. "Competing Technologies, Increasing Returns, and Lock-in by Historical Events." *The Economic Journal,* Vol. 99, No. 394 (March): pp. 116-31.

Babbage, Charles. 1835. *On the Economy of Machinery and Manufactures,* 4th ed. (London: Charles Knight).

Bagdikian, Ben. 1992. *The Media Monopoly,* 4th ed. (Boston: Beacon Press).

Bamford, James. 1982. *The Puzzle Palace: A Report on America's Most Secret Agency* (Boston: Houghton Mifflin).

Banfield, Edward C. 1958. *The Moral Basis of a Backward Society* (NY: The Free Press).

Bemer, R. W. 1969. "Position Paper for Panel Discussion—The Economics of Program Production." *Information Processing 68* (Amsterdam: North-Holland).

Bentham, Jeremy. 1797. *Panopticon, or the Inspection House.* in John Bowring, ed. *The Works of Jeremy Bentham,* 11 vols. (NY: Russell and Russell, 1962); vol. 4, pp. 37-172.

Berlan, Jean-Pierre. 1989. "The Commodification of Life." *Monthly Review,* Vol. 41, No. 7 (December): pp. 24-30.

Bernays, Edward L. 1928. *Propaganda* (NY: Liveright).

Bernstein, Lawrence and Christine Yuhas. 1989. "Software Manufacturing." *Unix Review,* Vol. 7, No. 7 (July): pp. 38-45.

Bernstein, Nina. 1997. "Lives on File: Privacy Devalued in Information Economy." *New York Times* (12 June).

Bhagwati, J. 1984. "The Splintering and Disembodiment of Services and Developing Nations." *The World Economy,* Vol. 7, No. 2 (June): pp. 133-43; reprinted in his *Wealth and Poverty,* vol. 1 of his *Essays in Development Economics,* Gene Grossman, ed. 2 vols. (Cambridge: MIT Press): pp. 93-103.

Bluestone, Barry and Stephen Rose. 1997. "Overworked and Underemployed: Unraveling an Economic Enigma." *The American Prospect,* No. 31 (March-April): pp. 58-69.

Brandt, Richard with Evan I. Schwartz and Neil Gross. 1991. "Can the U.S. Stay Ahead in Software: America Still Dominates the Market, but Foreign Rivals Threaten." *Business Week* (11 March): pp. 98-105.

Braunstein, Yale. 1981. "Information as a Commodity: Public Policy Issues and Recent Research" in *Information Services: Economics, Management, and Technology,* ed. Robert M. Mason and John E. Creps, Jr. (Boulder: Westview Press).

Braverman, Harry. 1974. *Labor and Monopoly Capital* (New York: Monthly Review Press).

Brecher, Jeremy and Tim Costello. 1994. *Global Village or Global Pillage: Economic Reconstruction from the Bottom Up* (Boston: South End Press).

Bridges, William. 1994a. *Job Shift: How to Prosper in a Workplace Without Jobs* (NY: Addison Wesley).

Bridges, William. 1994b. "The End of the Job." *Fortune* (19 September): pp. 62-74.

Broad, William J. 1994. "U.S. Begins Effort to Recast the Law on Atomic Secrets." *New York Times* (9 January): p. 1.

Brody, Herb. 1995. "Internet@crossroads.$$$." *Technology Review,* Vol. 94, No. 8 (May/June): pp. 24-31.

Brooks Jr., Frederick P. 1975. *The Mythical Man-Month: Essays in Software Engineering* (Reading, Mass.: Addison-Wesley).

Bumiller, Elisabeth. 1996. ASCAP Tries to Levy Campfire Royalties From Girl Scouts and Regrets It." *New York Times* (17 December).

Campbell-Kelly, Martin and William Aspray. 1996. *Computer: A History of the Information Machine* (New York: Basic Books).

Cantillon, Richard. 1755. *Essai sur la nature du commerce en general,* Henry Higgs, ed. (New York: Kelley, 1964).

Card, David and Alan B. Krueger. 1996. "Labor Market Effects of School Quality: Theory and Evidence." National Bureau of Economic Research Working Paper No. 5450 (February).

Carnoy, Martin. 1994. *Faded Dreams: The Politics and Economics of Race in America* (NY: Cambridge University Press).

Carroll, Paul B. 1987. Computer Glitch: Patching Up Software Occupies Programmers and Disables Systems." *Wall Street Journal* (22 January): pp. 1 & 12.

Castells, Manuel. 1996. *The Information Age: Economy, Society and Culture.* Vol. 1. *The Rise of the Network Society* (Oxford: Blackwell).

Center for Workforce Development. 1998. *The Teaching Firm: Where Productive Work and Learning Converge: Report on Research Findings and Implications,* Monika Aring and Betsy Brand, Project Directors (Newton, MA: Education Development Center, Inc., January).

Commission on the Skills of the American Workforce. 1990. *America's Choice: High Skills or Low Wages: The Report of the Commission on the Skills of the American Workforce* (NY: National Center on Education and the Economy).

Commoner, Barry. 1981. *The Closing Circle: Nature, Man and Technology* (NY: Knopf).

Costlow, Tim. 1996. "Software Explosion Rattles Car Makers." *Electronic Engineering Times,* (28 October): pp. 1 and 156-8.

Cowan, Robin and Philip Gunby. 1996. "Sprayed to Death: Path Dependence, Lock-In and Pest Control Strategies." *The Economic Journal,* Vol. 106, No. 436 (May): pp. 521-42.

Cox, Reavis. 1946. "Non-Price Competition and the Measurement of Prices." *The Journal of Marketing,* Vol. 10, No. 4 (April): pp. 370-83.

Cumby, Robert. 1996. "Forecasting Exchange Rates and Relative Prices with the Hamburger Standard: Is What You Want What You Get With McParity? National Bureau of Economic Research Working Paper No. 5675).

Cusumano, Michael A. 1991. *Japan's Software Factories: A Challenge to U.S. Management* (Oxford: Oxford University Press).

David, Paul A. 1975. "The "Horndal Effect" in Lowell, 1834-56: A Short-run Learning Curve for Integrated Cotton Textile Mills." in *Technical Choice, Innovation and Economic Growth: Essays on American and British Experience in the Nineteenth Century* (New York: Cambridge University Press): pp. 175-91.

————. 1985. "Clio and the Economics of QWERTY." *American Economic Review,* Vol. 75, No. 2 (May): pp. 332-37.

Day, Kelly and George B. Frisvold. 1992. "Medical Research and the Management of Genetic Research." Western Economic Association Meetings (SF, 12 July).

De Palma, Anthony. 1991. "Universities' Reliance on Companies Raises Vexing Questions in Research." *New York Times* (17 March).

Dowie, Mark. 1995. "Introduction." John C. Stauber and Sheldon Rampton. 1995. *Toxic Sludge is Good For You: Lies, Damn Lies and the Public Relations Industry* (Monroe, ME: Common Courage Press): pp. 1-4.

Doyle, Andrew. 1997. "Moving Target: Software Problems Are Delaying the Completion of the World's Most Advanced Air-Traffic-Control Centre." *Flight International* (21 May): pp. 26-27.

The Economist. 1996a. "Survey of the World Economy." (28 September): pp. 1-46.

The Economist. 1996b. "Inside Information." (29 June): p. 24.

Eliot, T. S. 1934. *The Rock: A Pageant Play* (London: Faber & Faber).

Ewan, Stuart. 1996. *PR: A Social History of Spin* (NY: Basic Books).

Foucault, Michel. 1979. *Discipline and Punish* (NY: Vintage).

Feder, Barnaby J. 1996. "Weather Forecasts Can Be Crucial for Business." *New York Times* (22 October).

Ferguson, Adam. 1793. *An Essay on the History of Civil Society,* 6th ed., Duncan Forbes, ed. (Edinburgh: Edinburgh University Press, 1966).

Feynman, Richard Phillips. 1988. *What Do YOU Care What Other People Think?* (NY: Norton).

Flynn, Laurie. 1987. "Borland Nearly Triples Price of Reflex for Mac." *Infoworld* (27 July) p. 5.

Franklin, Benjamin. 1771. "Letter to Jonathan Shipley (19 August)." in Benjamin Franklin. 1959. *The Papers of Benjamin Franklin,* Leonard W. Larabee and William B. Wilcox, eds. (New Haven: Yale University Press): vol. 18, pp. 208-11.

Freudenheim, Milt. 1997. "HMOs at Odds With Teaching Hospitals." *New York Times* (20 May).

Friedman, Milton. 1953. "The Case for Flexible Exchange Rates." in *Essays in Positive Economics* (Chicago: University of Chicago Press): pp. 157-203.

———. 1962. *Capitalism and Freedom* (Chicago: University of Chicago Press).

Galarza, Ernesto. 1977. *Farm Workers and Agri-business in California, 1947-1960* (Notre Dame: University of Notre Dame Press).

Galbraith, John Kenneth. 1967. *The New Industrial State* (Boston: Houghton Mifflin).

———. 1994. *A Journey Through Economic Time: A Firsthand View* (Boston: Houghton Mifflin).

Garfinkel, Simson. 1995. "A Prime Patent: Legal Rights to a Number Upset Programmers and Lawyers." *Scientific American,* Vol. 273, No. 1 (July): p. 30.

Gates, Bill. 1995. *The Road Ahead* (New York: Viking).

Gibbs, W. Wayt. 1994. "Software's Chronic Crisis." *Scientific American,* Vol. 271, No. 3 (September): pp. 86-95.

———. 1995. "Information Haves and Have-Nots." *Scientific American,* Vol. 272, No. 5 (May): pp. 12-4.

———. 1996. "The Price of Silence." *Scientific American,* Vol. 274, No. 4 (November): pp. 15-6.

Gilder, George. 1989. *Microcosm: The Quantum Revolution in Economics and Technology* (NY: Simon and Schuster).

Gordon, David M. 1978. "Capitalist Development and the History of American Cities." in William K. Tabb and Larry Sawers (eds.) *Marxism and the Metropolis: New Perspectives in Urban Political Economy* (New York: Oxford University Press): pp. 25-63.

———. 1996. *Fat and Mean: The Corporate Squeeze of Working Americans and the Myth of Managerial Downsizing* (NY: New Press).

Gore, Daniel. 1976. "Farewell to Alexandria." in *Farewell to Alexandria: Solutions to Space, Growth, and Performance Problems of Libraries,* ed. Daniel Gore (Westport, Conn.: Greenwood Press): pp. 164-80.

Graaf, J. de V. 1957. *Theoretical Welfare Economics* (Cambridge: Cambridge University Press).

Grossman, Lawrence. 1995. *The Electronic Republic: Reshaping Democracy in the Information Age* (NY: Viking).

Grossman, Sanford. 1981. "An Introduction to the Theory of Rational Expectation Under Asymmetric Information." *Review of Economic Studies,* Vol. 68, No. 154, pp. 541-59.

Grover, Ronald. 1996. "Patent Nonsense: All the (Copy)right Moves." *Business Week* (20 May): p. 6.

Gupta, Anil K. 1990. "Survival Under Stress in South Asia: A Socio-Ecological Perspective On Farmer Risk Adjustment and Innovations." *Capitalism, Nature, Socialism,* No. 5 (October): pp. 79-94.

Hagerty, Bob. 1991. "Elsevier to Buy Maxwell's Scientific Publishing Unit." *Wall Street Journal* (29 March): p. B8.

Halonen, Doug. 1994. "Malone: Few Will Rule Superhighway." *Electronic Media* (31 January): p. 31.

Hamilton, Joan. 1990. "Who Told You You Could Sell My Spleen?" *Business Week* (23 April): p. 38.

Harvey, David. 1995. "Globalization in Question." *Rethinking Marxism,* Vol. 8, No. 4 (Winter): pp. 1-18.

Hayek, Friedrich A. 1941. *The Pure Theory of Capital* (Chicago: Midway Reprint, 1975).

———. 1945. "The Use of Knowledge in Society." *American Economic Review,* Vol. 35, No. 4 (September): pp. 519-30.

———. 1946 "The Meaning of Competition." in *Individualism and Economic Order* (London: Routledge, 1948): pp. 92-106.

———. 1967a. "Notes on the Evolution of Systems of Rules of Conduct." *Studies in Philosophy, Politics and Economics* (Chicago): pp. 66-81.

———. 1967b. "The Economy, Science, and Politics." *Studies in Philosophy, Politics and Economics* (Chicago: University of Chicago Press): pp. 251-69.

Hays, Dennis. 1989. *Behind the Silicon Curtain: The Seduction of Work in a Lonely Age* (Boston: South End Press).

Haywood, Trevor. 1995. *Info-Rich and Info-Poor: Access and Exchange in the Global Information Society* (London: Bowker-Sauer).

Haywood, William and Bohn, Frank. nd. *Industrial Socialism* (Chicago); cited in Montgomery 1979.

Hegel, G.W.F. 1807. *Phenomenology of Spirit,* trans. A. V. Miller (New York: Oxford University Press).

Henderson, Rebecca and Iain Cockburn. 1996. "Scale, Scope, and Spillovers: The Determinants of Research Productivity in Drug Discovery." *Rand Journal of Economics,* Vol. 27, No. 3 (Spring): pp. 32-59.

Hettige, Hemamala, Robert E. B. Lucas, and David Wheeler. 1992. "The Toxic Intensity of Industrial Production: Global Patterns, Trends, and Trade Policy." *American*

Economic Review, Vol. 82, No. 2 (May): pp. 478-81.

Hirschman, Albert. 1984. "Against Parsimony: Three Easy Ways of Complicating Some Categories of Economic Discourse." *American Economic Review,* 74: 2 (May): pp. 89-95.

Hirshleifer, Jack. 1971. "The Private and Social Value of Information and the Reward to Inventive Activity." *American Economic Review,* Vol. 61, No. 4 (September): pp. 561-74.

———. 1987. *Economic Behavior in Adversity* (Chicago: University of Chicago Press).

Honan, William H. 1995. "Many U.S Schools Are Unsafe." *New York Times* (2 February): Sec. A, p. 7.

Hoxie, Robert Franklin. 1915. *Scientific Management and Labor* (New York: Augustus M. Kelley, 1966).

Hymer, Stephen. 1972. "The Multinational Corporation and the Law of Uneven Development." in Jagdish Bhagwati, ed. *Economics and the World Order* (London: Macmillan): pp. 113-40; reprinted in Richard D. Edwards, Michael Reich, and Thomas E. Weisskopf, *The Capitalist System: A Radical Analysis of American Society,* 2d. edn. (Englewood Cliffs, NJ: Prentice Hall, 1977) pp. 492-99.

Itoh, Makoto. 1995. *Political Economy for Socialism* (NY: St Martin's Press).

Jacoby, Russell. 1994. *Dogmatic Wisdom: How the Culture Wars Divert Education and Distract America* (NY: Anchor Books).

Jenkins, Holman W. 1996. "Don't Hate Me Because I Am Beautiful." *Wall Street Journal* (31 December): p. 23.

Judis, John B. 1986. "Software Prices." *In These Times* (3-9 September) pp. 16-17.

Jussawalla, Meheroo. 1988. "Information Economics and the Development of Pacific Countries." in Meheroo Jussawalla, Donald M. Lamberton and Neil D. Karunaratne, eds. *The Cost of Thinking: Information Economies in Ten Pacific Countries* (Norwood: NJ): pp. 15-43.

Kanigel, Robert. 1997. *The One Best Way: Frederick Winslow Taylor and the Enigma of Efficiency* (New York: Viking).

Kapor, Mitch. 1989. "Talk to the Creative Strategies Research International Conference, Alliance Japan." *Microtimes* (30 October): pp. 44-50.

Kerwin, Ann Marie. 1993. "Advertiser Pressure on Newspapers is Common: Survey." *Editor & Publisher* (16 January): pp. 28-9 and 39.

Keynes, John Maynard. 1927. "Liberalism and Industry: Address to the London Liberal Candidates Association at the National Liberal Club." reprinted in Donald Moggridge (ed.), *The Collected Works of John Maynard Keynes,* XIX, *Activities 1922-1929: The Return to Gold and Industrial Policy,* Part II (London: Macmillan, 1981): pp. 638-48.

———. 1931. "An Economic Analysis of Unemployment." in Philip Quincy Wright, ed. *Unemployment as a World-Problem: Lectures at the Harris Foundation,* (Freeport, New York: Books for Libraries Press, 1931): pp. 3-43; reprinted in Donald Moggridge, ed. *The Collected Works of John Maynard Keynes,* XIII, *The General Theory and After,* Part I, *Preparation* (London: Macmillan, 1973), pp. 343-67.

Kilborn, Peter T. 1996. "Factories That Never Close Are Scrapping 5-Day Week." *New York Times* (4 June): p. A1.

Kirzner, Israel M. 1988. "The Economic Calculation Debate: Lessons for Austrians." *The Review of Austrian Economics,* Vol. 2, pp. 1-18.

Kletke, P. R., D. W. Emmons, and K. D. Ellis. 1996. "Current Trends in Physicians' Practice Arrangements: From Owners to Employees." *Journal of the American Medical Association,* Vol 276, No. 7 (21 August): pp. 555-60.

Knecht, G. Bruce. 1997. "Hard Copy: Magazine Advertisers Demand Prior Notice of 'Offensive' Articles." *Wall Street Journal* (30 April): p. A1.

Kozol, Jonathan. 1991. *Savage Inequalities: Children in America's Schools* (NY: Crown).

Kremer, Michael. 1993. "The O-Ring Theory of Economic Development." *Quarterly Journal of Economics,* Vol. 58, No. 3 (August): pp. 551-76.

Krugman, Paul. 1992. "The Right, The Rich, and the Facts: Deconstructing the Income Distribution Debate." *American Prospect* (Fall): pp. 19-31.

Kuttner, Robert. 1997. *Everything For Sale: The Virtues and Limits of Markets* (NY: Alfred A. Knopf).

LaDou, Joseph. 1984. "The Not-So Clean Business of Making Chips." *Technology Review* (May/June).

Lagnado, Lucette. 1996. "Famed Cancer Center Gives In to Managed Care." *Wall Street Journal* (25 October): p. B 1.

Lavoie, Don. 1990. "Computation, Incentives, and Discovery." In *Privatizing and Marketing Socialism, Annals of the American Academy of Political and Social Science,* ed. J. Prybyla (London: Sage): pp. 72-79.

Lazonick, William and Thomas Brush. 1985. "The 'Horndal Effect' in Early U.S. Manufacturing." *Explorations in Economic History,* Vol. 22, No. 1 (January): pp. 53-96.

Levy, David. 1988. "The Market for Fame and Fortune." *History of Political Economy,* Vol. 20, No. 4 (Winter): pp. 615-25.

Lewis, Neil A. 1994. "A Debate Rages Over Disclosure of U.S. Secrets." *New York Times* (14 January): Sec. A, p. 11.

Liebowitz, S. J. and Stephen E. Margolis. 1990. "The Fable of the Keys." *Journal of Law and Economics,* Vol. 33, No. 1 (April): pp. 1-26.

Livingston, James. 1987. "The Social Analysis of Economic History and Theory: Conjectures on Late Nineteenth-Century American Development." *American Historical Review,* Vol. 92, No. 1 (February): pp. 69-95.

Lundberg, Erik. 1961) *Productivitet och Rantabilitet* (Stockholm: Norstedt & Soner).

MacIntyre, Alasdair C. 1984. *After Virtue: A Study in Moral Theory,* 2nd ed. (Notre Dame: University of Notre Dame Press).

Magner, Denise K. 1996. "To Many Science Ph.D's?" *The Chronicle of Higher Education* (15 March): pp. A19 and A20.

Mandel, Michael J. 1996. *The High-Risk Society: Peril and Promise in the New Economy* (NY: Times Books).

Marshall, Alfred. 1920. *Principles of Economics: An Introductory Volume,* 8th ed. (London: Macmillan & Co.).

———. 1923. *Industry and Trade: A Study of Industrial Technique and Business Organization; Of their Influences on the Conditions of Various Classes and Nations,* 4th ed. (London: Macmillan & Co.; NY: Augustus M. Kelley, 1970).

Marx, Karl. 1861-1863. *Economic Manuscript of 1861-3* in Karl Marx and Friedrick Engels. *Collected Works,* vol. 30. *Marx: 1861-1863* (New York: International Publishers, 1988).

———. 1862. "Letter to Engels, 20 August 1862." in Karl Marx and and Frederick Engels. *Collected Works,* vol. 41. *Marx and Engels: 1860-1864* (New York: International Publishers, 1988): pp. 410-12.

———. 1963-1971. *Theories of Surplus Value,* 3 Parts (Moscow: Progress Publishers).

———1977. *Capital,* Vol. 1 (New York: Vintage).

McGouldrick, P.F. 1968. *New England Textiles in the Nineteenth Century, Profits and Investment* (Cambridge, Massachusetts: Harvard University Press).

McMillen, Liz. 1991. "Quest for Profits May Damage Basic Values of Univerities, Harvard's Bok Warns." *Chronicle of Higher Education,* No. 32 (24 April): Sec. B, p. 8.

Melloan, George. 1994. "Keep the Information Superhighway a Freeway." *Wall Street Journal* (16 May): p. A19.

Merges, Robert P. 1995. "The Economic Impact of Intellectual Property Rights: An Overview and Guide." *Journal of Cultural Economics,* Vol. 19, No. 2, pp. 103-17.

Mill, John Stuart. 1848. *Principles of Political Economy with Some of Their Applications to Social Philosophy.* Vols 2-3. Collected Works, J. M. Robson, eds. (Toronto: University of Toronto Press, 1965).

Minkler, Alanson P. 1993. "The Problem with Dispersed Knowledge: Firms in Theory and Practice." *Kyklos,* 46: 4, pp. 569-87.

Mishel, Lawrence and Jared Bernstein. 1994. *The State of Working America, 1994-95* (Armonk, NY: M.E. Sharpe).

Montgomery, David. 1979. *Workers' Control in America: Studies in the History of Work, Technology, and Labor Struggles* (Cambridge: Cambridge University Press).

———. 1987. *The Fall of the House of Labor: The Workplace, the State, and American*

Labor Activism, 1865-1925 (Cambridge: Cambridge University Press).

Morgenstern, Oskar. 1935. "Perfect Foresight and Economic Equilibrium." in Andrew Schotter, ed. *Selected Writings of Oskar Morgenstern* (NY: New York University Press, 1976): pp. 169-83.

———. 1963. *On the Accuracy of Economic Observations,* 2d ed. (Princeton: Princeton University Press).

Mosco, Vincent. 1988. "Introduction: Information in the Pay-per Society." Mosco, Vincent and Janet Wasco, eds. 1988. *The Political Economy of Information* (Madison: University of Wisconsin Press).

Mukerjee, M. 1994. "Wall Street: Refugees from Physics Find Joy as 'Derivatives Geeks'." *Scientific American,* Vol. 271, No. 4 (October): pp. 126 and 128.

Narin, Francis, Kimberly S. Hamilton and Dominic Olivastro. 1997. "The Increasing Linkage between U.S. Technology and Public Science." *Research Policy,* forthcoming.

Naysmith, James. 1852. "Letter to Leonard Horner." (November); reprinted in Report of the inspectors of factories to Her Majesty's Principle Secretary of State for the Home Department for the Half Year ending 31st October 1856ò (London: HMSO, 1857).

Nelson, Richard and Sidney Winter. 1982. *An Evolutionary Theory of Economic Change* (Cambridge, MA: Belknap University Press).

Neumann, Peter. 1995. *Computer Related Risks* (Reading, MA: Addison-Wesley).

New York Times. 1996. "Former Student in Patent Fight Leaves Prison." (14 June): p. A 14.

Niggle, Christopher J. 1988. "The Increasing Importance of Financial Capital in the U.S. Economy." *Journal of Economic Issues,* Vol. 22, No. 2 (June): pp. 581-88.

Noble, David F. 1984. *Forces of Production: A Social History of Industrial Automation* (NY: Alfred A Knopf).

North, Douglass. 1981. *Structure and Change in Economic History* (NY: Norton).

Organisation for Economic Cooperation and Development. 1996. *The Knowledge Based Economy;* exerpted from *1996 Science, Technology and Industry Outlook* (Paris: OECD).

Packard, Vance Oakley. 1981. *The Hidden Persuaders* (NY: Pocket Books).

Pakes, Ariel and Griliches, Zvi. 1984. "Estimating Distributed Lags in Short Panels with an Application to the Specification of Depreciation Patterns and Capital Stock Constructs." *Review of Economic Studies,* Vol. 51, No. 2 (April): pp. 243-62.

Pakko, Michael R. and Patricia S. Pollard. 1996. "For Here or To Go? Purchasing Power Parity and the Big Mac." *Review of the Federal Reserve Bank of St. Louis,* Vol. 78. No. 1 (January/February): pp. 3-22.

Perelman, Michael A. 1977. *Farming for Profit in a Hungry World: Capital and the Crisis in Agricultural* (Totowa, NJ: Allenheld, Osmun).

———. 1991. *Information, Social Relations, and the Economics of High Technology* (NY and London: St. Martin's and Macmillan, 1991).

Perrow, Charles. 1984. *Normal Accidents: Living with High-Risk Technologies* (NY: Basic Books).

Petroski, Henry. 1989. *The Pencil: A History of Design and Circumstances* (NY: Knopf).

Phillips, Kevin. 1994. *Arrogant Capital: Washington, Wall Street, and the Frustration of American Politics* (Boston: Little, Brown).

Piore, Michael J. 1968. "The Impact of the Labor Market upon the Design and Selection of Productive Techniques within the Manufacturing Plant." *Quarterly Journal of Economics,* Vol. 82, No. 4 (November): pp. 602-20.

Porat, Marc Uri. 1977. *The Information Economy: Definition and Measurement,* Publication 77-12 (Washington D.C.: US Department of Commerce, Office of Telecommunications).

Postman, Neil. 1992. *Technopoly: The Surrender of Culture to Technology* (NY: Knopf).

Putnam, Robert, 1995. "Bowling Alone." *Journal of Democracy,* Vol, 6, No. 1 (January): pp. 65-78.

Ramstad, Evan. 1997. "DSC Won't Pay a Penny for His Thoughts." *Wall Street Journal* (14 July): Sec. B, p. 4C.

Ranney, Elizabeth. 1985. "The Puzzle of Software Pricing." *Info World,* Vol. 7, No. 44 (4 November) pp. 35-9.

Reid, T.R. and Hume, Brit. 1988. "Version 4.0 Makes MS-DOS Likable Bit of Software." *Sacramento Bee* (22 August): p. D6.

Rifkin, Jeremy. 1995. *The End of Work: The Decline of the Global Labor Force and the Dawn of the Post-Market Era* (NY: G.P. Putnam's Sons).

Ritzer, George. 1996. *The McDonaldization of Society: An Investigation Into the Changing Character of Contemporary Social Life,* rev. ed, (Newbury Park, Ca.: Pine Forge).

Robbins, Lionel Charles. 1969. *An Essay on the Nature and Significance of Economic Science,* 2d edn. (London: Macmillan).

Rosenthal, Elisabeth. 1997. "U.S. to Pay New York Hospitals Not to Train Doctors, Easing Glut." *New York Times* (2 February): p. A1.

Ross, Edward Alsworth. 1908. *Social Psychology* (NY).

Rulon-Miller v. International Business Machines (1985) 162 Cal. App. 3d, 241.

Sabel, Charles F. 1993. "Studied Trust: Building New Forms of Cooperation in a Volatile Economy." *Human Relations,* Vol. 46, No. 9, pp. 1133-70.

Sassen, Saskia. 1991. *Global City* (Princeton, NJ: Princeton University Press).

Schiller, Dan. 1988. "How to Think About Information." in Mosco, Vincent and Janet Wasco, eds. 1988. *The Political Economy of Information* (Madison: University of Wisconsin Press): pp. 27-43.

Schiller, Herbert I. 1985. "Supply-Side Knowledge: Information—A Shrinking Resource." *The Nation* (28 December): p. 708.

———. 1995. *Information Inequality: The Deepening Social Crisis in America* (NY: Routledge).

——— and Schiller, Anita R. 1988. "Libraries, Public Access to Information, and Commerce." in Vincent Mosco and Janet Wasco (eds.) *The Political Economy of Information* (Madison: University of Wisconsin Press): pp. 147-66.

Schor, Juliet B. 1991. *The Overworked American: The Unexpected Decline of Leisure* (NY: Basic Books).

Schultz, Theodore. 1961. "Investment in Human Capital." *American Economic Review,* Vol. 51, No. 1 (March): pp. 1-17.

Scitovsky, Tibor. 1945. "Some Consequences of the Habit of Judging Quality by Price." *Review of Economic Studies,* Vol. 12, No. 2, pp. 100-5.

———. 1991. "Hindsight Economics." *Banca Nazionale del Lavoro,* No. 178 (September): pp. 251-70.

Shaiken, Harley. 1985. *Work Transformed: Automation and Labor in the Computer Age* (NY: Holt, Rinehart & Winston).

Silvestri, George T. 1996. "Occupational Employment to 2005." *Monthly Labor Review,* Vol. 118, No. 11 (November): pp. 60-84.

Slawson, David. 1981. *The New Inflation* (Princeton: Princeton University Press).

Smith, Adam. 1976. *An Inquiry into the Nature and Causes of the Wealth of Nations,* R. H. Campbell and A. S. Skinner, eds. (New York: Oxford University Press).

———. 1978. *Lectures on Jurisprudence,* R. L. Meek, D. D. Raphael, and P. G. Stein, eds. (Oxford: Clarendon University Press).

Smith, R. Jeffrey. 1994. "32,400 Workers Stockpiling U.S. Secrets." *Washington Post* (15 May): p. 1.

Snoddy, Raymond. 1996. "McGraw-Hill: Business Journals to Launch on Internet." *Financial Times* (17 October).

Soley, Lawrence C. 1995. *Leasing the Ivory Tower: The Corporate Takeover of Academia* (Boston: South End Press).

Spink, Lynn. 1997. "Right to Poverty: Fear and Loathing at a Fraser Institute Right to Work Conference." *This Magazine* (Canada) 30: 4 (January/February): pp. 20-1.

Stahlman, Mark. 1995. "The Big Picture: Being Human In Digital Age." Information-Week (6 March): p. 73.

Stauber, John C. and Sheldon Rampton. 1995. *Toxic Sludge is Good For You: Lies, Damn*

Lies and the Public Relations Industry (Monroe, ME: Common Courage Press).

Stecklow, Steve. 1994. "At Phoenix University Class Can Be Anywhere—Even in Cyberspace." *Wall Street Journal* (12 September): p. 1.

Stephan, Paula. 1996. "The Economics of Science." *Journal of Economic Literature*, Vol. 34, No. 3 (September): pp. 1199-1262.

Stephan, Paula E. and Sharon G. Levin. 1992. *Striking the Mother Lode in Science: The Importance of Age, Place, and Time* (NY: Oxford University Press).

Stigler, George J. 1961. "The Economics of Information." *Journal of Political Economy*, Vol. 69, No. 3 (June): pp. 213-25.

Stiglitz, Joseph E. 1987. "The Causes and Consequences of the Dependence of Quality on Price." *Journal of Economic Literature*, Vol. 25, No. 1 (March) pp. 1-48.

———. 1994. "Endogenous Growth and Cycles." in Yuichi Shionoya and Mark Perlman, eds. *Innovation in Technology, Industries, and Institutions: Studies in Schumpeterian Perspectives* (Ann Arbor: University of Michigan): pp. 121-56.

———. 1995. *Whither Socialism?* (Cambridge: MIT Press).

Strrosnider, Kim. 1997. "An Aggressive, For-Profit University Challenges Traditional Colleges Nationwide." *The Chronicle of Higher Education* (6 June): pp. A32-A33.

Summers, Lawrence H. and Victoria P. Summers. 1989. "When Financial Markets Work too Well: A Cautious Case for a Securities Transactions Tax." *Journal of Financial Services Research,* Vol. 3, Nos. 2 and 3 (December): pp. 261-86.

Sylos-Labini, Paolo. 1983-84. "Factors Affecting Changes in Productivity." *Journal of Post Keynesian Economics,* Vol. 6, No. 2 (Winter): pp. 161-79.

Taylor, Frederick Winslow. 1911. *The Principles of Scientific Management* (New York: Norton).

———. 1947. *Scientific Management, Comprising Shop Management, The Principles of Scientific Management and Testimony Before the Special House Committee* (NY: Harper).

Tenenbaum, David. 1996. "Dvorak Keyboards: The Typist's Long-Lost Friend." *Technology Review,* Vol. 99, No. 5 (July): pp. 21-3.

Thompson, Edward P. 1963. *The Making of the English Working Class* (New York: Vintage).

Tucker, Josiah. 1758. *Instructions for Travellers* (Dublin: William Watson); reprinted in Kress-Goldsmith Microfilm Collection, Reel 712, Item 9323.

United Nations Development Programme. 1993. United Nations Human Development Report, 1993 (NY: Oxford University Press).

———. 1995. United Nations Human Development Report, 1995 (NY: Oxford University Press).

United States Senate. Select Committee on Intelligence. 1976. *Foreign and Military*

Intelligence (Washington, D.C.: U.S. Government Printing Office).

Varian, Hal. 1995. "Information Economy: How Much Will Two Bits Be Worth in the Digital Marketplace?" *Scientific American,* Vol. 273, No. 3 (September): pp. 201-2.

Veblen, Thorstein. 1898. "Why is Economics Not an Evolutionary Science?" *Quarterly Journal of Economics,* Vol. 12, No. 4 (July): pp. 373-97; reprinted in Max Lerner, ed. *The Portable Veblen* (NY: Penguin Books, 1977): pp. 215-40.

———. 1921. *The Engineers and the Price System* (NY: A. M. Kelley, 1965).

———. 1923. *Absentee Ownership* (NY: Viking).

Walker, Jerry. 1991. "Survey Shows PR People Have Media Clout." *O'Dwyer's PR Services Report* (September): p. 36.

Wall Street Journal. 1996a. "American Online Faces Lawsuit by NBA Over Data on Games." (29 August): p. B14.

Wall Street Journal. 1996b. "Girl Scouts Don't Have To Pay Fees To Sing Songs, ASCAP Said." (27 August): p. B2.

Wallis, J. J. and Douglass C. North. 1986. "Measuring Transaction Costs in the American Economy, 1870-1970." in Stanley L. Engerman and Robert G. Gallman, eds. *Long Term Factors in American Economic Growth.* National Bureau of Economic Research. *Studies in Income and Wealth,* vol. 51 (Chicago: University of Chicago Press): pp. 94-148.

Wells, H. G. 1938. World Brain (London: Methuen).

Williamson, Oliver E. 1993. "Contested Exchange Versus the Governance of Contractual Relations." *Journal of Economic Perspectives,* Vol. 7, No. 1 (Winter): pp. 103-8.

Winter, Sidney G. 1982. "An Essay on the Theory of Production." in S. H. Hymans, ed. Economics and the World Around It (Ann Arbor: University of Michigan Press): pp. 55-91.

———. 1991. "On Coase, Competence, and the Corporation." *The Nature of the Firm* in Oliver E. Williamson and Sidney G. Winter, eds. (Oxford: Oxford University Press): pp. 179-95.

Wolff, Edward N. 1995. *Top Heavy: A Study of the Increasing Inequality of Wealth in America* (NY: Twentieth Century Fund Press).

Wolpert, Lewis, and Alison Richards. 1988. *A Passion for Science* (NY: Oxford University Press).

Wright, T. 1936. "Factors Affecting the Cost of Airplanes." *Journal of the Aeronautical Sciences,* Vol. 3, No. 4 (February): pp. 122-28.

Yourdon, Edward. 1992. *The Decline and Fall of the American Programmer* (Englewood Cliffs: Prentice Hall).

Zachary, G. Pascal. 1996. "Manpower To Offer Physicists As Temps." *Wall Street Journal* (27 November): pp. A2 and A14.

———. 1995. "Study Predicts Rising Global Joblessness." *Wall Street Journal* (22 February): p. A2.

Zuboff, Shoshana. 1988. *In the Age of the Smart Machines: The Future of Work and Power* (NY: Basic Books).

———. 1993. "The Emperor's New Information Economy." In Orlikowsku, Wanda J. Geoff Walsham, Matthew R. Jones and Janice deGross, eds. *Information Technology and Changes in Organizational Work* (London: Chapman and Hall).

Index